"In *Songs of the Savior—The Person, Life, and Work of Christ in All the Psalms,* Ken Hanko offers a remarkable contribution to biblical theology and Christian worship. With exegetical care and theological depth, he demonstrates how the Psalter unfolds the person and work of Christ—revealing Him as both God and Man, our true Prophet, Priest, and King. From His incarnation and humiliation to His suffering, betrayal, crucifixion, death, resurrection, and exaltation, Hanko traces the rich Christology woven throughout Israel's hymnbook. He also explores the types and foreshadowing of Christ that pervade the Psalms, showing how they prefigure the coming Redeemer and find their fulfillment in Him. This insightful work not only enhances our understanding of the Psalms as Messianic Scripture but also restores their rightful place as songs for the church today—teaching us to sing, pray, and worship with renewed appreciation for the gospel they proclaim."

—M. David Sills, Ph.D.

SONGS *of the* SAVIOR

The Person, Life, and Work of Christ in All the Psalms

KEN HANKO

LUCIDBOOKS

Songs of the Savior: The Person, Life and Work of Christ in All the Psalms

Published by Lucid Books in Houston, TX
www.LucidBooks.com

ISBN: 979-8-90344-014-6
eISBN: 979-8-90344-015-3

A Note from the Author About Scripture Quotations

Modern translations of the Bible have copyrights and limitations on the amount of material an author may quote without special permission. The language of the King James Version, which is public domain, may be beyond the reach of some readers. Therefore, I have chosen, with only a few exceptions, to use my own translations of the Scriptures in this book.

CONTENTS

PREFACE

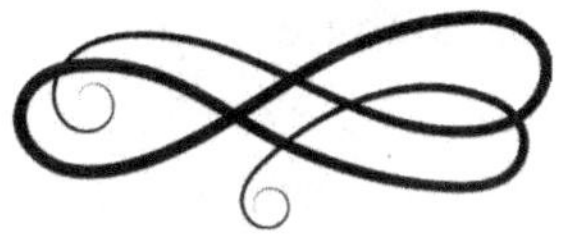

In *The Songs of Zion*, Michael Bushell quotes Martin Luther.

> The Psalter ought to be a precious and beloved book, if for no other reason than this: it promises Christ's death and resurrection so clearly—and pictures his kingdom and the condition and nature of all Christendom—that it might well be called a little Bible. In it is comprehended most beautifully and briefly everything that is in the entire Bible. It is really a fine enchiridion or handbook. In fact, I have a notion that the Holy Spirit wanted to take the trouble Himself to compile a short Bible and book of examples of all Christendom or all saints, so that anyone who could not read the whole Bible would here always have anyway an entire summary of it, comprised in one little book.[1]

[1] Michael Bushell, *Songs of Zion* (Pittsburgh: Crown and Covenant Publications, 1980), 93.

The Book of Psalms covers the whole scope of Christian doctrine: revelation (Ps. 19, 119); all the attributes of God such as power, righteousness, wisdom, and grace; and man in his original glory (Ps. 8) and fallen state (Ps. 14, 53). All of salvation is there: regeneration (Ps. 87), faith (Ps. 116), justification (Ps. 32, 51, 85, 130), sanctification (Ps. 15, 24), preservation (Ps. 23), eternal life (Ps. 36), and glorification (Ps. 17). Many psalms speak of the church both as the glorious house of God (Ps. 48, 87, 122, 125) and as the troubled and sinning people of God (Ps. 44, 81, 106). Even the last things are there, especially judgment (Ps. 96, 98) and the new creation (Ps. 8, 65).[2] As Martin Luther said, the Psalter is a little handbook of Christian teaching.

Yet this little handbook presents doctrine in a very personal and practical way. It shows us how it bears on our lives, whether its high mysteries trouble us or its strong truths sustain us. Bushell also quotes John Calvin:

> I have been accustomed to call this book, I think not inappropriately, "an anatomy of all the Parts of the Soul;" for there is not an emotion of which anyone can be conscious that is not here represented as in a mirror. Or rather, the Holy Spirit has here drawn to the life all the griefs, sorrows, fears, doubts, hopes,

---

[2] See also Frank L. Smith and David C. Lachman, eds., *Worship in the Presence of God* (Greenville Seminary Press, 1992), 200–201.

> cares, perplexities, in short, all the distracting emotions, with which the minds of men are wont to be agitated.[3]

Above all, the psalms reveal Christ. They reveal Him as God, creator, ruler, judge, and redeemer. They also reveal Him as man—like us in all things except sin, suffering bitterly, tempted sorely, and praying earnestly, but also as loving, obeying, rejoicing, hoping, and believing in God. His life and works appear to such an extent that getting just a glimpse of them will make us marvel. They show us not only Christ objectively but also Christ for the church (Ps. 125), for me as a member of the church (Ps. 122), and for the world (Ps. 96). He appears as authoritative teacher, mediator, bridegroom (Ps. 45), chief prophet, only high priest, eternal king, and atoning sacrifice (Ps. 22). Every aspect of His life and work—His names, natures, offices, and states—is in them.

The psalms, therefore, are an abundant resource for believers today. They can greatly enrich private, family, and public worship. While they instruct, they also give expression to the deepest joys and sorrows of life. They comfort, encourage, strengthen, warn, admonish, and rebuke. They set forth in personal terms the struggle against sin, the exultation of victory, and the hope of life.

"Every scribe instructed concerning the kingdom of

---

[3] Bushell, *Songs of Zion,* 93–94.

heaven is like a householder who brings out of his treasure *things* new and old" (Matt. 13:52). The psalms hold many treasures that shine more brightly in light of the New Testament than they ever could before He who fulfilled[4] all of them came.

[4] *Fulfilled* may mean three somewhat different things when used of Christ's fulfillment of the psalms. It may describe His fulfilling psalms that are specifically prophetic of Him. He was what the prophecies said He would be or did what they said He would do. Psalms 2 and 69 are examples. *Fulfilled* may also mean that His life and work extended the meaning of psalms that are not, at first glance, explicitly about Him. The Old Testament saints clearly understood God's work of judgment, but they may not have known that the exercise of that judgment would be by the promised Messiah. Finally, *fulfilled* may also mean simply that a psalm has its full meaning and applicability only in Christ. It applies also to His people only because He lived, prayed, and sang it as their Savior. Psalms 1, 8, and 64 are examples of this kind of fulfillment.

Chapter 1

CHRIST IN THE PSALMS

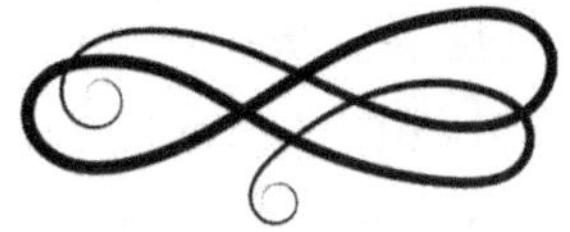

What place should the psalms have in the worship of the New Testament church? In the lives of Christians? Do they reveal the gospel, or are they relevant only to Old Testament times? Should the church replace them with hymns based on New Testament teaching? Should Christians ignore them as irrelevant to life under grace? Do they have anything to say about Christ?

If asked the last question, many Christians would speak readily of messianic psalms such as Psalm 2, 8, 16, 22, 23, 24, 40, 45, 68, 69, 72, 89, 110, and 118. These are mostly prophetic psalms, like Isaiah 53 in their descriptions of the Messiah's work. But is Christ in any psalms besides these?

Christ Is in the Psalms

On the road to Emmaus, the risen Lord opened the Scriptures for two disciples. "Beginning from Moses and from all the prophets, he interpreted to them in all the Scriptures the things concerning himself" (Luke 24:27). Surely, the psalms had their part in His discourse.

That same evening Jesus showed Himself to the disciples in the upper room. He rebuked them for failing to understand His teaching about Himself. "These are the words which I spoke to you while I was still with you, that it was necessary that all the things written in the law of Moses, and the prophets, and the Psalms concerning me should be fulfilled" (Luke 24:44).

The standard formulation for the Old Testament Scriptures is "the Law" or "the Law and the Prophets" This time Jesus singled out the psalms for special attention. Perhaps they, more than any other part of the Old Testament, reveal Him.

To distinguish some psalms as messianic implies that the rest are not. Nothing could be further from the truth. Our Lord Jesus Christ is in the psalms in a far richer way than we usually think.

Christ Used the Psalms in His Earthly Ministry

Jesus used the psalms during His earthly ministry. He taught from them, showed how they spoke of Him, sang them, and prayed them.

After the three leading groups among the Jews—the Pharisees, the Sadducees, and the Scribes—had tried to trip Jesus up with a hard question, He asked them a question based on Psalm 110: Why does David there call his son "Lord?" (Matt. 22:44). He was teaching them about His identity as both Son of God and son of David. On another occasion, when the Pharisees objected to the name "Son of God," Jesus quoted Psalm 82:6: "I have said, 'You are gods and all of you sons of the Most High'" (John 10:34). He whom the Father sent into the world has a right to be called "Son of God."

Later chapters will discuss in more detail Jesus' application of the psalms to Himself. Two more brief examples will suffice here. At the raising of Lazarus from the dead, Jesus prayed, "Father, I give thanks to you that you have heard me. And I knew that you always hear me (John 11:41–42)." Jesus was probably alluding to Psalm 118:21, a prophetic messianic psalm: "I will give thanks to you because you hear me." And in Matthew 11:25, Jesus gives thanks to His Father for hiding some things from the wise and prudent and revealing them to babes. "From the mouth of babies and nursing infants you have appointed strength" (Ps. 8:2).

Jesus also sang the psalms. He participated regularly in synagogue worship and in the three Jewish festivals where the psalms were sung. Probably the hymn that Jesus and the eleven sang before they went to the Mount of Olives (Matt. 26:30; Mark 14:26) was the Egyptian Hallel (Ps. 113–118). The Jews customarily sang it in their celebration of the

Passover. Hebrews 2:12 quotes from Psalm 22 to show that Jesus is not ashamed to call us brethren: "I will proclaim your name to my brethren. In the midst of the church I will hymn to you." Jesus fulfilled His preaching ministry partly by singing the psalms among His brethren.

Finally, Jesus prayed the psalms. The Gospels contain at least twenty references to Jesus praying. Sometimes the Scriptures record His words (cf. John 17; Matt. 11:25–26; John 12:27–28). But on the cross, He found no better way to express Himself than the psalms. Three of the seven cross-words derive from them. "I thirst" alludes to Psalm 69:21. "My God, my God, why have you forsaken me?" comes from Psalm 22:1. "Into your hands I commit my spirit" is a precise quotation of the Septuagint's rendering of Psalm 31:5. We may be sure that the whole content of these psalms was on His lips and in His heart, not only during His crucifixion but at many other times during His life of suffering.

During His life, Jesus made the psalms His own. He, as it were, took possession of them for Himself: "These are my songs, my prayers, my heart outpourings to my Father." Because we are one with Him, His use of them has made them ours. So He gave them to us not only by inspiration but also by using them Himself.

Different Kinds of Psalms Reveal Him

It is customary to divide the psalms into different kinds or categories, although commentators differ on what the categories are. For this chapter, the following will serve: prophetic psalms, royal psalms, historical psalms, creation psalms, wisdom psalms, psalms of suffering, psalms of confession of sin, and psalms of cursing.

It's easy to see Christ in the prophetic psalms and in those classified as royal psalms. He is the subject of the prophecy. He is the King. But what about some of the other categories?

The most prominent of the historical psalms are Psalms 78, 105, and 106. Psalm 78 recounts the reason for God's decision to move His house. Joshua had placed the tabernacle at Shiloh in Ephraim. Solomon built the temple in Jerusalem in the territory of Judah. There are at least two ways that Christ appears in it. He is the ultimate speaker: "Give ear, O my people, to my law" (v. 1). We must receive the psalm as a warning from our Lord that we, through faithlessness, may also come under the judgment of God. But He is also David (Ezek. 34:23–24; 37:24–25) chosen by the Lord "to shepherd Jacob His people and Israel His inheritance" (v. 71). Psalm 105 recalls God's covenant with Abraham: "to you I will give the land of Canaan" (v. 11). But Abraham inherited a better heavenly country by faith in that promise (Heb. 11:16). That country is the new creation that the Lord Jesus Christ will establish when He makes all things new (Rev. 21:5). Moses and Aaron both appear in Psalms 105 and 106 as prophetic foreshadowings of Christ our priest and intercessor. Psalm 106 is a confession of sin (v. 6) and a prayer for salvation. Believing Israel understood that forgiveness and salvation were in the promised

Messiah. They hoped for a better sacrifice than the law set before them.

Psalms 8, 19, 33, 65, and 104 describe God's glory in creation. "By the word of Yahweh the heavens were made" (Ps. 33:6). Jesus is the Word made flesh by whom all things were made (John 1:1–3).

The wisdom psalms (e.g., Ps. 119) are psalms of instruction in the ways of the Lord. Jesus learned obedience by the things He suffered (Heb. 5:8), and He is our wisdom (1 Cor. 1:30) and our instructor in His ways.

The psalms of suffering have their center in Christ, the subject of Chapter 5 of this book. The voice of the suffering servant of the Lord rises as clearly from them as from His cries from the cross. And when Yahweh answered His prayers, Jesus sang the psalms of thanksgiving and praise. He loved the city and house of God (Ps. 26, 48, and many others) and mourned with all His people when they fell into apostasy and oppression (Ps. 137). All our sorrows were His, and He knew all the anguish to which the bitterest psalms give expression.

Two categories raise difficult questions. May we say that the psalms of confession of sin belong to Him who knew no sin? It can be true only in a qualified sense. He was the spotless Lamb of God—holy, harmless, and undefiled. He never had to confess sin (Heb. 7:26–28). Yet the New Testament uses very strong language about His bearing our sins: God made Him "to be sin for us" (2 Cor. 5:21). He was condemned as a sinner and received that sentence as the judgment of God (John 19:10–11). He took the curse and condemnation of sinners on Himself. Therefore, He could sing and pray the psalms that confess sin and cry for deliverance from wrath (e.g., Ps. 6, 32, 38, 51). At the very least, in these psalms Jesus is asking that His Father turn away His wrath and forgive the sins of His people.

The other category is the imprecatory psalms, especially such strongly imprecatory psalms as 109 and 137. We find it hard to imagine that our Lord could pray, "Let his days be few, and let another take his office" (Ps. 109:8) or "O daughter of Babylon, laid waste, blessed is he who repays you as you rewarded us" (Ps. 137:8). Yet Peter applied the words of Psalm 109 to Judas Iscariot (Acts 1:20), and Jesus Himself pronounced devastating woes on the Pharisees and Jerusalem (Matt. 23). He is not only the Savior but also the God of vengeance (Ps. 94).

Conclusion

Christ is in the psalms in His deity and humanity; His suffering and glory; His prayers and praises; by the foreshadowing ceremonies of the law; and as our brother, our mediator, and our God. The psalms are varied, containing praise, instruction, admonition, prayer, prophecy, history, and law. By them God speaks to us and we to God, to each other, and to the nations. Christ's presence in them varies accordingly, but He is there if only we have eyes to see. He is there, not just in a few prophetic and messianic psalms but in all of them. He made them His own during His earthly ministry. We can grasp that only tenuously, but it should be our goal to understand them and sing them with Him as members of His body. They express the full range of human experience and emotion, from death to life and from deepest sorrow to abundant joy. They were His experiences and His emotions, and they become ours because of Him.

He is in all of them, either as one with us in our humanity or as our Savior and our God. He talked from them and by them sang of Himself, the Father, and the Spirit. He encouraged and admonished His brethren using their words and expressed through them His own deep need of His Father's help in the difficult work of doing His Father's will in the world. To neglect the psalms is to leave buried incalculable treasure. In them we not only learn about Christ but also hear His own prayers and meditations. We see His inner spiritual life in a way that we cannot in any other part of Scripture.

Chapter 2
GOD AND MAN

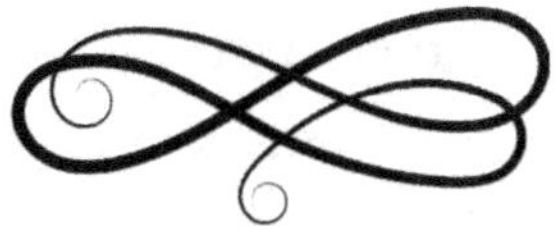

Christians confess that Jesus is both God and man. The Book of Psalms abundantly reveals Him as both.

The Psalms Reveal Christ as God

In the Book of Psalms, the name of Jesus can often and without distorting the meaning take the place of the name Yahweh. However, two comments are in order.

First, possibility does not imply necessity or preference. Isaac Watts believed that the psalms required christianizing and therefore used the name of Jesus often in his psalm adaptations (e.g., "Jesus Shall Reign Where'er the Sun"). That diminishes the meaning rather than enriching it. We lose the evidence of the unity of Christ with His Father. He said, "I and my Father are one." Substituting the name "Jesus" makes that unity disappear.

Second, this correspondence is not universal. As the

Athanasian Creed confesses, Jesus is "equal to the Father as touching His Godhead, and inferior to the Father as touching His manhood." Some psalms reveal Him as God. Others distinguish between Christ (the Anointed or the Messiah) and Yahweh, or between God and Jesus the obedient man.

"Kings of earth set themselves, and rulers sit in conclave together against Yahweh, and against His Anointed" (Ps. 2:2). The Lord responds to them: "I have installed my king upon Zion my holy hill" (v. 6). The Anointed declares the decree: "Yahweh has said unto Me, You are my Son; today I have begotten You" (v. 7).

The psalm differentiates between the Lord and the Anointed, yet the distinction is not absolute. The psalmist instructs the kings and judges to serve the Lord (v. 11) and to kiss the Son (v. 12). The acts are equivalent; kissing the Son is serving the Lord because the Son is the Lord.

Psalm 20 is a song of the people (or the priest) blessing the king before battle. The "you" is singular: "The Lord hear thee in the day of trouble; the name of the God of Jacob defend thee" (v. 1, KJV). The king is David, but David as prefiguring Christ. The blessing came to Christ from the Lord in part through John's baptism and the gift of the Holy Spirit. And the church today still blesses Him: "To him who sits upon the throne and to the Lamb blessing and honor and glory and might forever and ever" (Rev. 5:13).

Psalm 21:1–3 delineates the blessings the Anointed received.

O Yahweh, in your strength the king will rejoice...
The desire of his heart you have given to him...
You will meet him with blessings of goodness.
You will set on his head a crown of pure gold.

Later verses blur the clear distinction between the Lord and the king made in earlier verses. Of whom do verses 8–12 speak: the king or the Lord? "Your hand will find all your enemies." It doesn't really matter; there is essential unity between them.

One final example: Psalm 118:22–23 prophesies:

The stone which the builders have rejected
Is the head of the corner.
This is from Yahweh;
It is a wonder in our eyes.

Jesus identified Himself with that stone in Matthew 21:42.

However, while some psalms make a distinction between Christ and Yahweh, others equate them. His name is Jesus, "Yahweh saves." He is God. He commands worship. To apply some psalms about the Lord directly to Christ does not distort their meaning. Rather, it acknowledges that in Jesus, the Lord tabernacles among men. Christ is God manifest in the flesh.

Many psalms celebrate the Lord as King; Jesus is that King. Hebrews 1:8–9 uses Psalm 45:6 to affirm Christ's deity: "Your throne, O God, is forever and ever: A scepter of uprightness is the scepter of your kingdom." Yet the same psalm calls him King under God. "You love righteousness and hate wickedness: Therefore God, your God, has anointed you with the oil of gladness above your companions."

This is the wonder of the incarnation, that one who is God and equal with God is also man and King under God.

Similarly, Ephesians 1:20–21 recalls the words of Psalm 99:3. Jacob's holy God is none other than the Lord Jesus Christ.

And the strength of the king loves judgment;
You establish uprightness.
You perform judgment and righteousness in Jacob.
Exalt Yahweh our God and worship at his footstool.
Holy is he!

Psalm 147:3 foresees the power of God working through Jesus during His earthly ministry to perform miracles. Verse 6 extols His compassion for the humble. But if verses 3 and 6 are about Jesus, are not verses 4 and 5 also?

He counts the number of the stars;
He calls them all by name.
Great is our Lord, and abundant in power:
His understanding is beyond reckoning.

And who would think of Jesus in connection with these verses? Psalm 102:25–27 says:

Of old you have laid the foundation of the earth,
And the heavens are the work of your hands.

They will perish, but you will endure,
And all of them like a garment will wear out.
As clothing you will change them,
And they will change,
But you are the same,
And your years will not end.

Hebrews 1:10–12 applies that passage directly to Christ.

These verses from Psalm 102 also reveal that Jesus is the Creator. Psalm 33:6 does the same. According to John 1:1, the Word of the Lord that brought the creation into existence is a person, the Word who became flesh and dwelt among us. Even the Spirit appears here. "Breath" in the second part of the verse— "and by the breath of his mouth all their host"—in both Hebrew and Greek can also mean spirit, and the Hebrew word is a name for the Spirit of God.

Other psalms reveal Jesus as God the Lord in different ways. In Psalm 17:15, David says to the Lord, "As for me, in righteousness I will behold your face. I will be satisfied when I awake with your likeness." That is the Old Testament equivalent of 2 Corinthians 3:18: "But we all with uncovered faces beholding as in a glass the glory of the Lord, are transfigured into the same image from glory unto glory, just as by the Lord the Spirit." And of 1 John 3:2: "Beloved, now we are children of God, and not yet is it manifest what we will be, but we know that, when He is manifested, we will be like Him, for we will see Him as He is."

At the time David wrote Psalm 17, he knew that he would

see the face of God. He has now seen it because the risen Lord has ascended into heaven and sits at God's right hand.

In John 10, Jesus describes Himself as the good shepherd. He is the Lord of Psalm 23: "Yahweh is my shepherd." Psalm 19:14, as interpreted by comparison with a multitude of other scriptures, shows him as the Lord our strength and our redeemer. Psalm 36:7–9 describes Him as the water of life and the light.

When He comes as judge at the end of time, Jesus will fulfill all the psalms that talk about God as judge (Ps. 7, 9, 11, and many others), for the Father has committed all judgment to the Son (John 5:22). Many psalms speak of God as Savior: Jesus is the One in whom this became true.

Many psalms set Jesus before us as God above all gods, worshipful king, omnipotent Savior, or righteous judge.

The Psalms Reveal Christ as Man

The psalms also reveal Jesus as man, both in His suffering and in His exaltation. Jesus was once a man in the world singing and praying psalms with His disciples. He was also, as our brother, leading the way through the valley of the shadow of death. He is now glorified man, exalted to the right hand of the Father, full of grace and truth, transforming us to the same glory.

Jesus is the righteous man of Psalms 1, 15, 24, and 26. He is the one whose delight was in the law of the Lord. He walked uprightly, worked righteousness, and spoke truth in

His heart. He had clean hands and a pure heart and did not lift His soul to vanity or swear deceitfully. He loved the habitation of the Lord's house and hated the congregation of evildoers. The church today can sing such psalms only because He has imputed His righteousness to her.

Jesus is a fellow sufferer in Psalm 7:3–4 because He too was falsely accused. He prayed in Psalm 9:13–14:

Be gracious to me, O Yahweh.
See my affliction from those who hate me,
You who exalt me from the gates of death,
That I may recount all your praise
In the gates of the daughter of Zion.
I will exult in your salvation.

Jesus was a reproach among His enemies and neighbors, and a fear to His acquaintances (Ps. 31:11). His enemies sharpened their tongues like swords and shot their bitter words like arrows (Ps. 64:3). He suffered everything that we suffer, and many times with greater intensity.

Psalm 8 uses language reminiscent of God's first work of creation but really prophesies about the new creation. Hebrews 2 uses the psalm to remind believers of the greatness of their salvation: "For to the angels he has not subjected the coming world of which we speak. But someone testified in a certain place saying, 'What is man? . . . You made him a little lower than the angels.'"

A couple of verses later the writer of Hebrews says, "But now we do not yet see all things subjected to him.

But we discern Jesus who was made a little lower than the angels . . . with glory and honor crowned."

Jesus was tempted in all points like His brothers, yet without sin. He was touched with the feeling of their infirmities. Afterward God exalted Him to be a sympathetic High Priest (Heb. 4:14–16). The psalms, therefore, speak of Jesus both in His humiliation and in His exaltation. He was a man like other men in everything except sin, and He is exalted now so we too may be crowned with glory and honor.

Conclusion

The psalms unfolded to the people of God in the Old Testament much of the doctrine of Christ. Jesus is both the God of our salvation whom we seek and worship and a man like ourselves, our older brother who suffered, praised, and prayed with us. Thus, He is our mediator. That is the subject of the next chapter.

Can we see Jesus as both God and man in the same psalm? Yes. Psalm 9, for instance, presents Him as the needy one whom the Lord will not forget (v. 18), but also as the judge (v. 5) and a refuge for the oppressed (v. 9). Part of the wealth of the Book of Psalms is exactly that we see Him, sometimes in the same psalm, both as our brother and as our God. He is indeed God with us.

Chapter 3

OUR PROPHET, PRIEST, AND KING

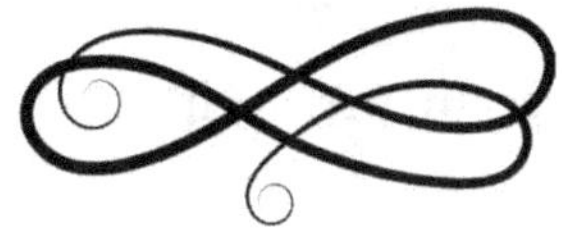

Jesus is God, co-eternal and co-equal with the Father; and He is man, one with us in His earthly life. He is also God and man in one person, appointed by God to be the mediator to reconcile His people to God. He is subordinate to God as the servant of the Lord, and at the same time exalted above us and indeed all creation. He has this glory by His anointing to be our Prophet, Priest, and King.

The offices of prophet, priest, and king existed in the Old Testament as separate functions. The prophets spoke the word of God to His people and to the world. The priests ministered in God's house, offering sacrifices, performing cleansings, and making intercession for the people. The kings ruled in God's name and on His throne.

All of them received anointing, and many of them received a pouring of oil that signified the gift of the Holy Spirit. The kings usually received it from one of the prophets.

The priests received it in a very elaborate ceremony from other priests. The prophets, with the exception of Elisha, received their calling directly from God, not through an anointing by men. God's call to any office bestowed the gift of the Holy Spirit (1 Sam. 10:6; 16:13; Isa. 6:1–8).

Kings and priests could also be prophets (e.g., David and Samuel), but kings might not serve as priests or priests as kings. When Uzziah, king of Judah, trespassed in this and tried to offer incense in the temple, God struck him with leprosy, thus banning him from the temple for the rest of his life (2 Chron. 26:16–21).

God also anointed our Lord Jesus Christ with His Spirit, as signified at Jesus' baptism when the Holy Spirit descended on Him in the form of a dove. His title (Christ in the Greek and Messiah in the Hebrew) designates Him as God's Anointed. He unites all three offices in Himself. Thus, He is Prophet, Priest, and King under God and for us.

Christ anoints all His people with the Spirit, so they are all—from the least to the greatest—prophets, priests, and kings under Him. This is the significance of Pentecost. Peter used the prophet Joel to explain the 120 people speaking in different languages:

> *And it will be in the last days, says God, I will pour out from my Spirit upon all flesh: and your sons and your daughters will prophesy, and your young men will see visions, and your old men will dream dreams: And also upon my male servants and upon my female servants in*

> *those days I will pour out from my Spirit; and they will prophesy.*
>
> —Acts 2:17–18

Peter also said, "But you are a chosen generation, a royal priesthood, a holy nation, a people for His possession; that you may publish the praises of Him who called you out of darkness into His marvelous light" (1 Pet. 2:9). Saints in the New Testament have a high honor that no one in the Old Testament, except Melchizedek, ever had.

Christ's anointing qualifies Him to be the mediator, who gives the blessing of anointing to us. Though there were mediators in the Old Testament, Jesus is special because He holds all three offices. He not only mediates between us and God but also represents reconciliation in the union of His two natures in the one person of the Son of God. He is both God and man, living as it were on both sides of the great gulf between them. But He also stands between God and man to work out salvation according to the purpose of His Father and for His glory. As Prophet, He revealed the whole counsel of God and through His messengers continues to speak even today. Moses spoke of Him in Deuteronomy 18:15–18 (cf. Acts 3:22–23):

> *A prophet from among you, from your brothers, like me, Yahweh your God will raise up for you—him you shall hear—according to all that you asked from Yahweh your God in Horeb in the day of the assembly, saying, "Let me not hear again the voice of Yahweh my God,*

and this great fire let me not see any more, that I may not die." And Yahweh said unto me, "They have done well in what they have spoken. A prophet I will raise up for them from among their brothers, like you, and I will give my words into his mouth; and he will speak unto them all that I will command him."

God fulfilled this prophecy in our Lord's incarnation and ministry. As Priest, Jesus offered Himself for our sins. Now, at the right hand of God, he intercedes for us daily to obtain for us all He merited by His death. As King, He rules us in grace, fights our battles, and makes us more than conquerors. The psalms reveal all of this.

The Psalms Reveal Christ as Prophet

The Book of Psalms' revelation of our Lord Jesus Christ as Prophet is an intricate and multi-layered thing that will require some careful distinctions and explanations.

First, He is the eternal Word of God so that all God's revelation of Himself comes through Jesus. He speaks God's word but also reveals God in His own person and works.

God who at various times and in various ways long ago spoke to the fathers in the prophets, in these last days has spoken to us in His Son, whom He appointed heir of all things, through whom also He made the ages; Who being the effulgence of the glory, and the replica of His

> *substance, and upholding all things by the speech of His power, through Himself having accomplished purification of our sins, sat down on the right hand of the Majesty in the heights, having become as much better than the angels as He has by inheritance obtained a more excellent name than they.*
>
> —Heb. 1:1–4

The passage does not even mention the words of Christ but rather describes who He is and what He has done. It is also in these that Christ serves as God's Prophet. When the psalms talk about who Christ is or what He has done, Jesus, the exact replica of His Father's substance, is revealing the God of our salvation.

Second, Christ as chief Prophet inspired the psalms (and all the Scriptures) so that in reading or singing the psalms, we are hearing His voice. He is the good shepherd. His sheep hear His voice. He knows them, and they follow Him.

Third, our Lord inspired the use of the psalms in the New Testament. He inspired Luke to include Peter's sermon on the Day of Pentecost (Acts 2). It interprets Psalm 16 as a prophecy of the resurrection. He also moved Paul to use Psalm 2 to prove the resurrection (Acts 13). Christ took His own word from the psalms and gave it to His apostles to repeat to their contemporaries. His inspired Scriptures transmit it to all subsequent generations.

Fourth, when our Lord used, prayed, and sang the

psalms during His earthly ministry, He was acting as God's Prophet. He said what He did for Himself—to understand His own experience in the world and express Himself to God and His fellow men—but also for His people. He spoke with a view to the scriptural records of His life and words. Thus, He inspired David the prophet to write Psalm 22:1: "My God, my God, why have you forsaken me?" On the cross He repeated it as the experience of His own utter desolation and for the benefit of those who stood by. Finally, for our sakes, He inspired the scriptures that record His crucifixion. By them we know that He is indeed the Lamb of God forsaken for us. He also inspired David to write Psalm 23, fulfilled it when He described Himself in John 10 as the Good Shepherd, and finally inspired the scriptural record of His explanation. That word was a guide to His own understanding of Himself, a manifesting of Himself to His contemporaries, and a revelation of Himself to us.

Therefore, the psalms display layers of revelation. Christ inspired the psalmists to write about many things, including Himself. The psalmists wrote them, and the people sang and prayed them. But then Christ came and spoke them again from His own experience and for the instruction of His contemporaries. He also gave them to His apostles to record in the Scriptures so we also could hear His voice.

Finally, we hear Christ's voice in the psalms in very special ways, in ways we do not hear Him in the rest of the Scriptures. The "I" of the psalms is often Christ Himself.

I will recount the decree:
Yahweh said unto me,
You are my Son;
Today I have begotten you.
Ask from me, and I will give
Nations as your inheritance,
And as your possession the ends of the earth.
You will break them with a rod of iron;
Like a potter's vessel you will shatter them.

—Ps. 2:7–9

He is not only speaking about Himself in the first person but also declaring what the Lord said to Him. That is a prophetic function.

Both as God and as Prophet of God, Christ inspired the psalmists to record words He would later speak and fulfill. David said, "Depart from me, all you workers of iniquity" (Ps. 6:8), but Jesus will say the same thing to the wicked who stand before His judgment seat (Matt. 7:23). Christ said, "I will proclaim your name to my brothers: In the midst of the church I will hymn to you" (Ps. 22:22, Heb 2:12). When He came into the world at His incarnation, Jesus humbled Himself:

Then I said, Behold, I come:
In the roll of the book it is written about me,
I delight to do your will, O my God,
And your law is in the midst of my inward parts.

—Ps. 40:7–8 (cf. Heb. 10:5–10)

David's complaint of betrayal (probably by Ahithophel) is also the complaint of our Lord Jesus Christ (Ps. 41:9; Ps. 55:12–14, Matt. 26:21–23, John 13:18). He said, "The zeal of your house has eaten me up, And the reproaches of those who reproached you have fallen on me" (Ps: 69:9 with John 2:17 and Rom. 15:3).

What kinds of things beyond what is recorded in the Gospels did Christ say during His earthly ministry? What were His daily prayers like? What were the thoughts He did not speak aloud? The Book of Psalms contains an enormous amount of information. They reveal His inner spiritual life in a way and to an extent that no other scriptures do. We have in them a spiritual biography of our Lord.

The words of the psalms, therefore, are the words of Christ in different ways. They are His inspired speech. They are very often His words as a man among men, singing and praying to His Father in heaven. They are His prophecies concerning Himself, especially in the messianic psalms. And they are sometimes His own unique voice as the Son of God in our flesh saying things only He could say.

The Psalms Reveal Christ as High Priest

The Heidelberg Catechism ascribes two functions to our Lord's high priestly office. He offered Himself as atonement for our sins, and He makes intercession for us.

The most important psalm regarding Christ's priesthood is Psalm 110. In it David distinguishes himself from his

Lord (the son promised to him in 2 Samuel 7) and his Lord from the Lord (or Yahweh). David describes in the psalm what Yahweh said to his Lord: "Sit at my right hand until I make your enemies your footstool." The psalm is about the royal power of Christ exercised against His enemies (He "will strike kings in the day of his anger") and about the participation of Christ's people in His spiritual battles ("Your people will be a free will offering in the day of Your might").

But in verse 4, the psalm takes us into the eternal counsel of God and to His oath to David's Lord that He will be a Priest forever after the order of Melchizedek. Christ, who was from the tribe of Judah, is a royal Priest and greater than any priest from the tribe of Levi. His priesthood is essential to His royal power and wars. By His sacrifice He conquered our enemies and united us to Himself in an unbreakable bond of love. From His position at the right hand of power He makes intercession for us (Rom. 8:35–39).

Nevertheless, the priesthood of Aaron was a foreshadowing of the greater priesthood of Christ. Therefore, the psalms that talk about Old Testament priests are also about Christ.

> *Let your priests be clothed with righteousness,*
> *And let your saints shout for joy . . .*
> *And her priests I will clothe with salvation,*
> *And her saints will shout aloud for joy.*
>
> —Ps. 132:9, 16

In Old Testament times, priests and saints were distinct groups of people. Because of Christ's priesthood, that is no longer true. Every saint is also a priest, clothed with the righteousness and salvation of the great High Priest. Psalm 51:19 promises to God the sacrifices of righteousness due Him for His saving work among His people. These are Christ's thank-offerings, but also ours (Rom. 12:1).

The most important psalm about the sacrificial aspect of Christ's work as Priest is Psalm 22. Chapter 6 of this book will discuss it in more detail, but foundational to its discussion is the reality of Christ's priesthood. The psalm does not mention priests or sacrifices but describes instead Christ's offering Himself for our sins. He was forsaken by His God and cried to Him for deliverance from the cross. In Psalm 27:1–4, our Lord sets for us a pattern of godly living. Enemies troubled Him; he turned to the Lord with confidence: "I will not be afraid." The Lord delivered Him, and He sought the one thing He desired: to dwell in the house of the Lord (the heavenly sanctuary) all His days, to behold the beauty of the Lord, and to inquire in His temple. Dwelling in the house of the Lord is a priestly privilege. In Psalm 66:13–15, Christ says:

> *I will come into your house with burnt offerings:*
> *I will pay to you my vows,*
> *Which my lips have uttered,*
> *And my mouth has spoken in my trouble.*
> *Burnt offerings of fatlings I will offer to you*

With the incense of rams;
I will bring an ox with goats.

—Ps. 66:13–15

Likewise in Psalm 116:16–18:

Truly, O Yahweh, I am your servant;
I am your servant, the son of your maidservant.
You have loosened my bonds.
To you I will sacrifice the sacrifice of thanksgiving,
And on the name of Yahweh I will call.
My vows to Yahweh I will pay
Now in the presence of all his people,
In the courts of the house of Yahweh,
In the midst of you, O Jerusalem.

The Book of Psalms also reveals Christ in His intercessory work. Psalm 99:6 lists Moses, Aaron, and Samuel (all priests) among those who called on the Lord. He answered them. And Psalm 106:23 describes Moses' intercession for Israel after the sin with the golden calf at Mount Sinai. Moses stood before the Lord in the breach and turned away his wrath. These priests were types of our Lord Jesus Christ in His priesthood. Their intercession represented the intercession of Christ for us and the blessings that follow. "Yahweh our God, you have answered them. You have been to them a God who forgives and who avenges their doings" (Ps. 99:8).

Some psalms record Christ's actual prayers for His people. Psalm 28:8–9 is an example. The psalm is a prayer of

David but also a prayer of Christ, and concludes with these words about God's people and their Anointed One:

Yahweh is strength to them.
The salvation of his Anointed is he.
Save your people, and bless your inheritance,
And shepherd them,
And bear them forever.

Whether the last is a prayer of the people or of the Anointed makes little difference. They pray together, and God's people pray in and through their Anointed Priest.

In Psalm 69:9 (as interpreted by John 2:17), Christ exercises another function of the priest: to cleanse the house of God from evildoers. In Psalm 77:20, 103:7, and 105:26 are further references to Moses and Aaron as leaders and shepherds of the people.

The Book of Psalms reveals Christ as Priest especially in the typical language of the Old Testament ceremonies and foreshadowing institutions.

The Psalms Reveal Christ as King

The Lord is King. Therefore, Christ as the second person of the Trinity, equal with the Father in everything, is King. But Christ is King also as man, exalted by God to sit at God's right hand and rule under Him over all things. Some psalms reveal Christ as the Lord, the King (Ps. 99), and some reveal Him as distinct from the Lord and King under

Him. This section addresses the latter: Christ's sitting at God's right hand. In this position, He is the enthroned Lamb, the Lion of Judah and the servant of the Lord who executes all God's purposes (Rev. 5) and rules in His name over all creation.

This may well be the most prominent theme in the Book of Psalms. David and his contemporaries wrote most of them when the Kingdom of Israel had become powerful and glorious. It is to be expected, then, that the psalms have much to say about that kingdom and its King. They reveal the king as ruler, warrior, judge, and establisher or restorer of the true worship of the Lord.

The title Son of God reveals Christ as God. The Jews took exception to it precisely because they understood that fact (John 10:33). But it also reveals Christ as the man raised from the dead and glorified to sit at God's right hand. The Lord declares of Him, "You are my Son. Today I have begotten you" (Ps. 2). And the Son cries, "You are my Father, my God, and the rock of my salvation" (Ps. 89:26).

The preceding chapter discussed Christ's kingship at some length; this discussion will pick up only a couple of additional points. First, the King appears very unexpectedly in several psalms. Psalm 28:8 is one example. The psalm is of David but is a personal and private prayer. Yet in verse 8, the Anointed suddenly appears as if from nowhere. Psalm 61 is similar. In verse 6, without prior warning, David confesses, "You will add days to the days of the king." In Psalm 63:11, the same thing happens again: "And the king shall rejoice in God." Psalm 84 is a prayer of longing for God's house, but verse 9 refers to the Anointed. These references seem to interrupt the flow. What is the point? The answer is that the people of God can never be separated from their King. What affects them affects the King, and what affects the King affects them. Their prayers are the King's prayers, His prayers are theirs; their songs His songs, and His songs theirs. The people never come to God apart from Him, and He never approaches God except on their behalf. In such a context, what seem to be unexpected references to the King are as natural as our referring occasionally to others in conversation with a friend.

Second, there are a few psalms that show Christ the King in a somewhat different light. Psalm 18 is David's celebration of all the victories the Lord had given him over his enemies, including Saul. In the prayer at the end of the psalm, David extends his confidence for himself to his descendants, among whom is Christ: "He makes great the salvations [the Hebrew is plural] of his king; and does lovingkindness to his anointed, to David, and to his seed for evermore." Psalm 72 is a description of the blessings of the Messiah's reign, especially the blessing of justice for the poor. Psalm 89:20 uses the name David, but this David is also our Lord Jesus (Jer. 30:9, Ezek. 34:23–24). And the sufferings of the anointed described in the same psalm, verses 38–51, are also the sufferings of Christ. Psalm 132 is not only a psalm about the priests but also about the king.

There will I cause the horn of David sprout:
I have ordained a lamp for My Anointed.
His enemies will I clothe with shame,
and upon Himself His crown will flourish.

Since David and Solomon were both types of Christ, we should pay special attention to their psalms. When they speak, they often speak as prefiguring Christ and with the words of their greater son.

Conclusion

Christ is our chief Prophet, our only High Priest, and our eternal King. The Book of Psalms reveals Him to us in all the glory and power of these three offices. When we study them, we are studying Christ and ourselves as united to Him by His mighty deeds. And when we glorify God in the psalms, we also glorify Christ the Lord's Anointed and our mediator.

Chapter 4

THE INCARNATION

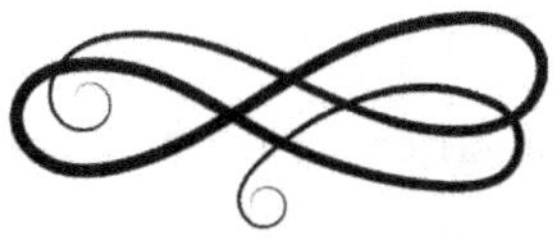

This chapter and the ones that follow will describe what the Book of Psalms says about the life of our Lord Jesus Christ in the state of humiliation and the state of exaltation.

The Apostles' Creed outlines five steps in the state of humiliation and four in the state of exaltation. Those in the state of humiliation are incarnation, suffering, crucifixion, death, and burial. Those in the state of exaltation are resurrection, ascension, sitting at the right hand of God, and coming again in judgment.

The incarnation is first.

What the Psalms Do Not Reveal

The doctrine of the incarnation consists of two chief parts. (1) The virgin Mary conceived by the power of the Holy Spirit. (2) This work of God in her resulted in the union of the divine and human natures of our Lord Jesus Christ in the person of the Son of God, the second person of the Trinity. By this grand work the one mediator between God and men is both God and man.

Several New Testament passages teach these things, especially the accounts of Jesus' birth in Matthew 1:18–2:12, Luke 1:26–38, and Luke 2:1–20. John 1:1–18, Philippians 2:6–7, and Colossians 1:15–18 have theological explanations of this great miracle. There is nothing as explicit or detailed as these found in the Book of Psalms.

There are also some Old Testament prophecies of the incarnation, especially Isaiah 7:14, Isaiah 9:6–7, and Micah 5:2–5. There is nothing in the psalms to compare with these passages.

What the Psalms Do Reveal

Nevertheless, there are three important things about the doctrine of the incarnation in the teaching of the Book of Psalms. The psalms, in alignment with the Lord's covenant with David, prophesy about a Son of David who will reign forever on David's throne and will even be Yahweh Himself (cf. Ps. 45, 72). Prior chapters described that. The full implications of that promise appear only in light of the New Testament's teaching about the incarnation. The second consists of specific passages in the Book of Psalms that the New Testament interprets as applying to the incarnation or indicates should be understood in light of the incarnation. The third consists of certain verses from the Book of Psalms whose meaning expands greatly when we see them through the lens of the incarnation.

Psalm 2

With regard to psalms whose implications become clear only in the New Testament, the first is Psalm 2:7: "Yahweh has said to me, 'You are my Son. Today I have begotten you.'" It describes the incarnation as well as the resurrection. When the wise men came to Jerusalem, they asked, "Where is he who has been born king of the Jews?" They were not looking for a prince but a king. When they found the King, they worshiped Him and offered Him royal gifts. They may have known the prophecy of Balaam in Numbers 24:17–19: "A star will march forth from Jacob. A scepter will rise from Israel. . . . From Jacob one will have dominion," or that of Micah 5. Furthermore, Jesus did not say, when asked by Pilate, that He would be a king but, "You say rightly that I am a king" (John 18:37).

Perhaps even the eternal generation of the Son, the second person of the Trinity, by the Father underlies the psalm. But that is outside the scope of this discussion.

Psalm 8

Hebrews 2 begins with a warning to us not to neglect the great salvation God has given. Christ spoke about it through His apostles and confirmed it by their signs, wonders, miracles, and gifts of the Holy Spirit. The author uses Psalm 8 to demonstrate how great this salvation is:

You have made him [man] a little lower than the angels.
With glory and honor you have crowned him,
And appointed him over the works of Your hands.
All things you have subjected under his feet.

But we do not yet see all things put under man. Instead, we see Jesus "who was made a little lower than the angels" now crowned with glory and honor. When the apostle applies the psalm to us, he is looking from the bottom up. God has exalted man to be a little lower than the angels. When he applies it to our Lord, he is looking from the top down. God has humbled Jesus and made Him a little lower than the angels. He has taken on the stature of a man. He has "emptied himself, having taken the form of a bondservant, having come in the likeness of men" (Phil. 2:7).

Psalm 40

According to Hebrews 10:5–10, Psalm 40:6–8 are words of our Lord Jesus Christ about His incarnation: "Having entered into the world, he says: 'Sacrifice and offering You did not want, but a body you have prepared for me' . . . Then I said, 'Behold, I come . . . O God, to do your will.'"

In the Hebrew there is no reference to a body. The New King James Version translates the Hebrew as "My ears

You have opened." "My ears you have dug out" would be better; the Hebrew word is the same one used in Genesis 26:25 for digging a well. "Opened" is very tame. "Dug out" is a vivid metaphor that suggests strongly the powerful creative activity of God in preparing His servant for a life of obedience.

In the book of Hebrews, the Holy Spirit gives more than a simple translation of the psalm; it is also an interpretation. The basic idea of "a body you have prepared" is the same as "my ears you have dug out." God called and prepared His servant for obedience. But the interpretation contained in the word *body* points emphatically to the incarnation. Christ came into the world. God prepared for Him a body. The purpose of this coming and this body was to do the will of God (v. 7) and to sanctify us "through the one time offering of the body of Jesus Christ" (v. 10).

Other Psalms

Psalm 80 is a prayer for the restoration of God's people: "Restore us, O God" (vv. 3, 7, 19). It anticipates that restoration will come through the man of God's right hand, "the son of man whom you have made strong for yourself" (Ps. 80:17). In the Gospels, Son of Man is a very common title for our Lord Jesus Christ. He is the ultimate restorer of God's people and, in His ascension, the man of God's right hand. God made Him strong for His work at least partly in the incarnation. That coming into our flesh qualified Him to be the mediator. "There is one mediator between God and men, the man Christ Jesus" (1 Tim. 2:5).

Two other verses that imply the incarnation are Psalm 86:16 and 116:16. David calls himself the son of God's maidservant. Because David was a type of Christ, this title can also apply to the Lord Jesus in His human nature. It is a more specific form of the title Son of Man. Mary said to Gabriel after the announcement of the virgin birth, "Behold the maidservant of the Lord! Let it be to me according to your word" (Luke 1:38).

Though Old Testament saints could not have developed the doctrine of the incarnation from these psalms, the Holy Spirit inspired them to anticipate the incarnation of the eternal Word and His dwelling among us.

Psalms Clarified in Light of the Incarnation

There are various statements throughout the Book of Psalms whose significance is more clearly understood and whose force is made greater in light of the incarnation. Psalm 103:14 is one such statement. In verse 13, David blesses the Lord for His compassion to His children, those who fear His name. In verse 14, he goes on to explain that the Lord is compassionate because "He knows our frame. He remembers that we are dust." The Lord created us in the beginning. He knows the limitations of our creatureliness. He also knows fully the effects of His curse: "Dust you are and to dust you shall return." When He judges us for sin, when He tests us, when strong temptations come our way, He takes pity on our weakness and frailty. He will not permit us to be tempted beyond what we can endure.

But the incarnation greatly enriches our understanding of His compassion. How does He know our frame? He knows it not only by His omniscience but because He has taken our frame upon Himself in His Son. He remembers that we are dust because He became dust with us. We have a sympathetic High Priest who, though He has passed through the heavens to be seated at God's right hand, was touched with the feeling of our infirmities and tempted in all points as we are, though without sin.

Psalm 113 is similar, though it uses very different language. The psalm praises the Lord who dwells on high, who is high above all nations, whose glory is above the heavens. But this same exalted Lord also "humbles Himself to see things in the heavens and in the earth." He doesn't just take the time to learn about our troubles. In His Son, He condescended to become a man among men, not a great man among the great but a man born in poverty, persecuted, rejected, betrayed, humiliated, and killed by His own people.

"Though Yahweh is high, yet He sees the lowly" (Ps. 138:6). "When my spirit is enfeebled within me, then you know my path. In the way in which I walked they have concealed a snare for me" (Ps. 142:3). The Lord Jesus knows our path because He walked there Himself and always had to be on the watch for the traps His enemies set for Him.

There are more psalms that would illustrate this point, but these examples will be an encouragement to look for them.

Conclusion

The people of God in the Old Testament could not have understood all the details of the doctrine of the incarnation from these psalms, not even with the addition of the wonderful prophecies from Isaiah and Micah. But they did understand that their God was with them, that their Redeemer, Savior, and King had come to dwell among them, and that this dwelling would be richer and more glorious as He continued to fulfill His covenant promises.

Neither could the people of God in the Old Testament understand the full depth of meaning in the psalms we discussed, but the essentials of understanding were there. The pouring out of the Spirit has given us a greater appreciation. How rich and glorious the psalms are! In what extraordinary ways they reveal to us our Savior! With what power they speak to us of the great work of salvation accomplished by the incarnate Son!

Chapter 5

LIFELONG SUFFERING

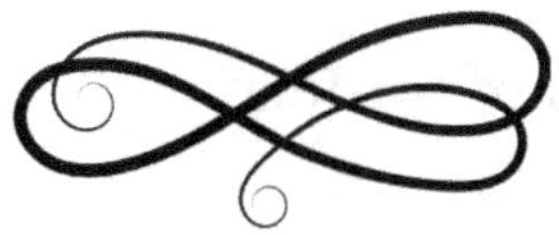

Suffering is a very prominent theme in the Book of Psalms. Approximately two-thirds of the psalms make direct reference to it. It is of all kinds and degrees, and from all sources. But the sovereign Lord determines the measure of suffering each person must endure, and He ultimately directs all suffering to His own ends.

Sometimes suffering comes by way of direct providential acts (e.g., when a hurricane destroys our property or a disease ravages our bodies). But sometimes He uses personal agents: enemies, family, and friends. The psalms talk of being forsaken by God and men, attacked in war, and falsely accused; suffering sickness, doubt, fear, old age, sorrow, and judgment for sin; enduring grief, loneliness, and temptation. They run the whole gamut of human sufferings and pain, from the mild to the severe, from hunger to death, from sickness to abandonment, from doubt to the most extreme sorrow. They are a tremendous source of comfort for all God's suffering people simply in giving them a way to give expression to their own troubles.

But the question for this chapter is this: How is Christ in the psalms of suffering? The answer to that question depends greatly on the kind of suffering a particular psalm has in view.

Different Kinds of Suffering

According to 1 Peter 2:20, there are at least two causes of suffering: suffering because of our faults and suffering because of the good we have done. On the one hand, the prophets threatened severe judgments on Israel because of their idolatry, and Paul warned the Corinthians that sickness and death among them came because of their abuse of the Lord's Supper (1 Cor. 11:30). On the other hand, Cain killed Abel because his own works were evil, and his brother's were righteous (1 John 3:12). The Jews persecuted Paul because of his faithfulness to the gospel of Christ.

But there are other reasons as well. The blind man in John 9 suffered so the works of God could be revealed in him (John 9:3), and 1 Peter 1 indicates that much of our suffering is for the purifying of our faith. Psalm 119:71 says, "It is good for me that I have been afflicted, That I may learn Your statutes." God uses suffering in many different ways.

Perhaps more than anything else, we suffer without knowing its reason. God has His purposes, and for His people those purposes are always good, but He often does not let us know them. This kind of suffering is the hardest to bear because it always leaves us with this question: Why?

Three kinds of suffering are especially prominent in the psalms: judgment for sin, persecution, and those adverse circumstances for which we have no explanation.

Our Suffering

The Book of Psalms speaks often of suffering for sin. Three examples will suffice. Psalm 6 begins, "O Yahweh, do not in your anger rebuke me, and do not in your fury chasten me." In Psalm 32 David says:

When I kept silent my bones grew old
In my roaring all the day.
For day and night your hand was heavy upon me.
My moisture is changed into the drought of summer.

Psalm 38 begins with the same words as Psalm 6 and then goes on:

Your arrows pierce me,
And your hand descends upon me.
There is no soundness in my flesh
Because of your indignation.
There is no peace in my bones because of my sin.

Persecution (suffering for righteousness) is also a common theme. One phrase that expresses this is "without cause." "Let those be ashamed who act treacherously without cause" (Ps. 25:3). "Without cause they have hidden for me a pit, their net. Without cause they have dug for my soul" (Ps. 35:7). "Do not let them rejoice over me, my enemies wrongfully, nor let those hating me without cause wink the eye" (Ps. 35:19). "They . . . fought against me without cause" (Ps. 109:3). "Princes persecute me without cause" (Ps. 119:161). "Without cause" means without just cause. The unjust cause is the enemy's hatred of God and of all that represents Him in this world.

Psalm 3 is a psalm of David when he was fleeing from Absalom. The supporters of Absalom said of him, "There is no salvation for him in God." Psalm 7 is a complaint against Cush, a Benjamite who had falsely accused David of repaying evil to someone who was at peace with him and plundering an enemy without cause (v. 4). There are many other examples of suffering for righteousness' sake.

Two questions found in the Book of Psalms point us to unexplained suffering. The first is "Why?" Psalm 10 is about persecution, but God's seeming unwillingness to help magnified the psalmist's suffering. "Why, O Yahweh, do you stand far off?" (v. 1). Psalms 42 and 43 are either one psalm that somehow was broken up in transmission or two psalms that are very closely related. In them is this question: "Why have you forgotten me? Why must I mourn in the oppression of the enemy?" Psalm 80:14 asks, "Why, O Yahweh, do you reject my soul? Why do you conceal your face from me?" These are personal psalms. Psalm 44 is a communal one. "Wake up! Why do you sleep, O Lord? . . . Why do you hide your face, and forget our affliction and our oppression?" (vv. 23–24). Psalm 74 is also communal and a lament for Jerusalem after its destruction by the Babylonians. The reason for the suffering is sin, but the people still ask for an explanation. It seems to them that judgment has gone too far.

This is the other question that arises in the context of unexplained suffering: "How long?" In these psalms, there may be an explanation for the suffering, but the psalmist feels that the suffering will never end.

And my soul is exceedingly disturbed.
But you, O Yahweh, how long?

—Ps. 6:3

How long, O Yahweh? Will you forget me perpetually?
How long will you hide your face from me?
How long will I take counsel in my soul,
Having sorrow in my heart daily?
How long will my enemy be exalted over me?

—Ps. 13:1–2

Lord, how long will you look on?

—Ps. 35:17

How long will you smoke against the prayer of your people?

—Ps. 80:4

> *How long will the wicked, O Yahweh, how long will the wicked triumph?*
>
> —Ps. 94:3

Psalm 79:5, 89:46–47, and 90:13 are additional examples.

Other psalms do not use the same questions but express the same anxiety.

> *Truly God is good to Israel,*
> *To the pure of heart.*
> *But I, my feet had almost stumbled,*
> *My steps had nearly slipped,*
> *Because I envied the boastful.*
> *I saw the peace of the wicked.*
>
> —Ps. 73:1–3

> *Forever will the Lord cast off,*
> *And will he not be favorable again?*
> *Has his lovingkindness ceased perpetually?*
> *Has his promise come to an end to generation after generation?*
> *Has God forgotten to be gracious?*
> *Has he shut down in anger his mercies?*
>
> —Ps. 77:7–9

Christ's Suffering and Ours

Our Lord Jesus suffered in all these ways. Though He did not have any personal sin, He bore our sins and suffered under the judgment of God for them. He also suffered many things for righteousness' sake. His enemies were always opposing His teaching, denying His miracles, and laying traps for His tongue. He said of them:

> *If I had not come and spoken to them, they would not have sin, but now they have no pretext for their sin. He who hates me also hates my Father. If I had not done among them the works which no one else has done, they would not have sin, but now they have both seen and also hated both me and my Father. But this happened so that the word might be fulfilled which is written in their law, "They hated me without a cause."*
>
> —John 15:22–25

His brothers did not believe in Him, His closest friends forsook Him, and Peter denied Him with cursing. Finally, He was tried, falsely accused, condemned, and unjustly sentenced to the worst possible death.

When Christ suffered for our sins, He entered into our sufferings. He took what in justice belongs to us. He who knew no sin became sin for us. And by this entering into our sufferings, He mitigates our own sufferings for sin. God does still judge us in many different ways for our sins, but His anger never destroys us. Christ has borne our destruction. He turns judgment in wrath to judgment in love, and condemnation to chastening.

When we suffer for righteousness, we enter into Christ's suffering. The apostles rejoiced that they were counted worthy to suffer for Christ's name (Acts 5:41). Paul counted all things loss and rubbish for the excellence of the knowledge of Christ, that he might know Him and the power of His resurrection and the fellowship of His suffering and be conformed to His death (Phil. 2:8–10). He filled up in his flesh what was lacking in the afflictions of Christ (Col. 1:24). In persecution we partake of Christ's sufferings (1 Pet. 2:12–13).

Even when we do not understand why God afflicts us, we know that Christ has suffered and been tempted in every way that we have. He has known our suffering in all its shapes and sizes. Therefore, He is a compassionate High Priest, and we may come boldly to the throne of grace to obtain mercy. He has become one with us and has made us one with Him so that both in suffering and glory we are partakers of the same things.

Christ's Suffering and Ours in the Psalms

When the psalmists complain about persecution from their enemies, they are partaking of the sufferings of Christ. Though they did not know it, they were joining their voices with the voice of their suffering and glorified Head in supplication to God. The anointed king of Israel foreshadowed in his person and in many events of his life not only the kingship but also the life and suffering of our Lord. When his heart was overwhelmed, David cried to God from the end of the earth (Ps. 61). He thirsted for God (Ps. 63), and Jesus was often in prayer to His Father for the same reason. Another psalmist (or perhaps David again) believed that the Lord would hear him because of His righteousness (Ps. 66:18–19), but he could do it only because he was in Christ. David's prayer in Psalm 86 is very personal, but it was also the prayer of Jesus:

> *O God, the presumptuous have risen against me,*
> *And the congregation of the ruthless have sought my soul*
> *And have not set you before them . . .*
> *Turn to me and be gracious to me.*
> *Give your strength to your servant,*
> *And save the son of your maidservant.*
>
> —Ps. 86:14–16

Satan quoted Psalm 91:11–12 to Jesus in one of his three attacks in the wilderness. He wanted Jesus to tempt God by throwing Himself down from a pinnacle of the temple. Jesus rejected the temptation, but the promise was as true for Him as it is for us. He made the Lord His refuge and dwelling place (v. 9), and the Lord gave His angels charge over Him to keep Him in all His ways (Matt. 4:11). The Word of God, the light of the world, came to His own, and His own people did not receive Him. They rejected the chosen and precious stone, but God made Him the head of the corner (Ps. 118:22; Matt. 21:42). The proud hid a snare for Him, but He cried to the Lord, and the

Lord covered His head in the day of battle (Ps. 140:5–7). He prayed:

Bring my soul from the dungeon
That I may give thanks to your name.
The righteous will surround me,
Because you will reward me.

—Ps. 142:7

The Lord was His rock and fortress who subdued His people under Him and rescued Him from the hand of foreigners (Ps. 144).

These psalms connect believers' suffering with the sufferings of Christ; they suffer for His sake and He for theirs. He endured the cross, and they bear it following Him.

A question arises. When the psalms make confession of sin (as in Psalms 6, 32, 51), are these confessions also the confessions of Christ? Yes, but with qualifications. Jesus cried out to God because of the heavy wrath of God He bore: "O Yahweh, do not rebuke me in your anger" (Ps. 6:1). That's very similar to "Let this cup pass from me." He was made sin for us and was judged and condemned as a sinner. He even received His judgment as coming from God. The qualification is, of course, that though He was made sin, He was not a sinner (Heb. 4:15, 7:26).

Our Lord understood His suffering much better than we understand ours. His suffering was, in some sense, all under the wrath of God. Yet there was at least one occasion when He did not understand why He suffered. When He cried,

"My God, my God, why have you forsaken me?" (Ps. 22:1), He was so troubled by the heavy hand of God that at that moment He did not understand the purpose of His death. Yet He remained obedient.

There are limitations to other aspects of this fellowship of suffering. We cannot enter into the full experience of His suffering for sin precisely because He bore the judgment that belonged to us. We may feel forsaken, but we have the assurance that "when my father and my mother forsake, then the Lord will gather me in" (Ps. 27:10). He was utterly forsaken. Some of the saints have suffered very painful deaths at the hands of their enemies, perhaps Peter was crucified, but none has suffered such a painful death as our Lord under God's curse. Our suffering is limited because Jesus bore the fullness of God's wrath for us.

And Jesus does not enter fully into the experience of our sin. He knew the power of temptation. When Satan wanted Jesus to turn stones into bread, He was hungry. When Jesus asked that the cup pass, His soul was in great terror. But He never sinned or desired sin, and never in thought or desire rebelled against the will of His Father.

Conclusion

This fellowship of suffering, Christ with us and we with Christ, given such vivid expression in the Psalms, is an immeasurable comfort to us in all our sorrows. He bore our judgment so judgment will not destroy us. We endure persecution with Him and rejoice to be counted worthy to suffer for His name. And when we do not understand the heavy trials God sends, still we know that He knows our frame and remembers that we are dust. He is a merciful and faithful High Priest who suffered temptation so He is able to help those who are being tempted (Heb. 2:18).

Chapter 6
THE CRUCIFIXION

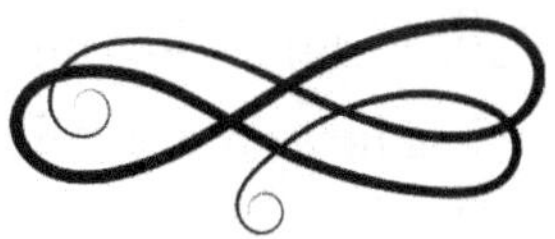

The crucifixion of our Lord Jesus Christ rightly permeates our thinking about Him. It is one of the few facts about Jesus that nearly everyone, Christian and non-Christian alike, knows. It is also a significant part of New Testament teaching. Yet crucifixion is not nearly as prominent in the Old Testament. It is certainly clear from passages such as Isaiah 53 that the Messiah must suffer and die, but there is little about the manner of His death. Even the passage the Apostle Paul quotes in Galatians 3:13 does not say anything about crucifixion as a means of death. It only specifies that the body of one who has been hung on a tree (not a cross) after death must be removed and buried before the end of the day.

> *And if there shall be in a man a sin liable to death, and he is put to death, and you hang him on a tree, his corpse shall not remain overnight upon the tree, but you shall certainly bury him on that day (for accursed*

of God is one hanged), and you shall not defile your land which Yahweh your God is giving to you as an inheritance.

—Deut. 21:22–23

Only two or three passages mention the practice in Israel. The first is Joshua 8:29. Joshua hung the body of the king of Ai on a tree, removed it just after sundown, and covered it with a heap of stones. He did the same thing with the bodies of the five kings of the Amorites (Josh. 10:26–27). In these two crucifixions it is evident that the hanging of their bodies signified the curse of God. 2 Samuel 4:12 may contain a third reference. David executed the murderers of Ishbosheth (the son of and short-lived successor to Saul), cut off their hands and feet, and hanged them by the pool in Hebron. There is no reference to burial either before or after the end of the day.

The Book of Psalms does not reveal the manner of our Lord's death any more than the rest of the Old Testament. But read in light of the New Testament, it does divulge certain circumstances related to Jesus' crucifixion and sets before us at least one prayer that comes close to a description of the scene.

Psalms Fulfilled in the Crucifixion

The New Testament alludes to various psalms in its descriptions of and references to the crucifixion. The church in

Jerusalem understood that the crucifixion of our Lord fulfilled Psalm 2.

> *Who through the mouth of David your servant said, "Why did nations rage, and peoples contrive vain things? The kings of the earth stood by, and the rulers gathered together against the Lord and against his Christ." For truly against your holy servant Jesus, whom you anointed, both Herod and Pontius Pilate, with the nations and the people of Israel, were gathered together, to do whatever your hand and your counsel predetermined would happen.*
>
> —Acts 4:25–28

Any righteous king of Israel could have said this. Many nations have risen against the church in both Old and New Testaments. But the culmination of all Satan's efforts was at the cross. There especially he gathered all the hosts of darkness to suppress once and for all the kingdom of God and devour the child of the woman (Rev. 12:4). And there at the cross were representatives of both the world and the church, all united in their deadly purpose. At the cross more than anywhere before or since, the kings of the earth set themselves against the Lord's Anointed, and there more than anywhere the Lord held them in derision. What they thought was victory, He turned into the defeat from which they will never recover.

In His trials, our Lord suffered at the hands of many false witnesses. They testified that He intended to destroy the temple, that He was perverting the people, forbidding to pay taxes, claiming to be a king to challenge Caesar, and stirring up the people. Jesus fulfilled the words of the psalmist in Psalm 27:12: "Against me rise false witnesses, and those who breathe out violence" and Psalm 35:11: "Violent witnesses rose up. What I do not know they asked."

Psalm 34:20 promises that the Lord guards all the bones of the righteous. "Not one of them is broken." This looks back in part to the Passover. The people of Israel were not to break any bones of the Passover lamb (Num. 9:12; Exod. 12:46), but it also looks ahead to the crucifixion. John said:

> *But having come to Jesus as they saw that He had already died, they did not break His legs. But one of the soldiers with a spear pierced His side, and immediately blood and water came out. And he who saw has testified, and his testimony is true: and he knows that he speaks truth, that you may believe. For these things happened so that the scripture should be fulfilled, A bone of Him shall not be broken. And again another scripture says, "They will look on Him whom they pierced."*
>
> —John 19:33–37

This little incident is one more confirmation that Jesus is the Lamb of God who takes away the sin of the world. But why did God command Israel not to break the bones of the Passover lamb? Why must Jesus' bones be preserved from such damage? The breaking of bones may signify a complete destruction. Our Lord did not suffer complete destruction.

By His resurrection, He escaped the breaking of His bones and the corruption of His body.

During the hours of His suffering on the cross, Jesus cried, "I thirst!" And those who were there gave him sour wine to drink (Matt. 27:34, 48; Mark 15:23, 36; Luke 23:36; John 19:29). In receiving that wine, Jesus fulfilled Psalm 69:21: "And they gave me for food gall, And for my thirst they caused me to drink vinegar."

Many other verses in Psalm 69 also point to the crucifixion. "More than the hairs of my head Are those who hate me without cause" (v. 4, cf. John 15:25). "Because for your sake I have borne reproach; Shame has covered my face" (v. 7; cf. Matt. 27:39–44). "A stranger am I to my brothers, A foreigner to the sons of my mother" (v. 8). His brothers did not believe and the twelve forsook Him. "The zeal of Your house has consumed me" (v. 9; cf. John 2:17). It was His zeal for God's house that made Him willing to offer the temple of His body for the church, which is also His body and the house of God. "Let their encampment be desolated. In their tents let no one dwell" (v. 25; cf. Acts 1:20).

Psalm 88 is the most sorrowful of all the psalms. There is no relief or hope of relief in it. The only positive thing about it is that the psalmist is crying to the God of his salvation, though he seems to cry in vain. Such suffering was especially characteristic of our Lord on the cross.

My life touches sheol . . .
You set me in the pit of the lower parts,

In darkness, in the depths.
On me rests Your indignation,
And with all your breakers You afflict me.
You have put far away from me those who know me.
You have made me an abomination to them.
I am shut up and do not come forth. . . .
For the dead will You do a wonder?
Will the deceased arise and give thanks? . . .
Why, O Yahweh, do You cast off my soul?
Why do You hide Your face from me?
Over me Your fury passes.
Your terrors annihilate me.

—Ps. 88:3, 6–8, 10, 14, 16

How are we to understand Jesus' use of these psalms? Some of them (e.g., Ps. 16:8–11, 22) are directly prophetic and have no immediate reference to other persons. In others we hear the voice of an Old Testament messiah (especially David) crying out with words that also became the words of Christ Himself (Ps. 2, 69). Sometimes Jesus simply found in the psalms the words He needed to give expression to His own pain and sorrow (Ps. 31:15; 41:9). But even in the last of these, Christ was the One who fulfilled them, because just as He was the firstborn from the dead, so He was the first sufferer. Our suffering as the people of God is always in fellowship with Him.

Psalm 22

There is one psalm that stands out above all others as the psalm of the crucifixion. It is Psalm 22. The first part of the psalm is both a prayer of the Son to the Father in His desolation and a detailed description of the scene at Golgotha.

The psalm has two parts (vv. 1–21 and vv. 22–31), sharply divided by the last line of verse 21: "You have answered me." The first part is about suffering; the second is about response to deliverance.

The first part has two main sections, and each ends with the petition: "Be not far from me" (vv. 11, 19–21). Verses 1–11 describe especially internal suffering or spiritual anguish, and verses 12–21 describe physical suffering caused by enemies.

Verses 1–11 consist of three stanzas and the concluding petition. In verses 1–3 is the cry of desolation; in verses 3–5 the psalmist contrasts the fathers' trust and deliverance with His own forsakenness; in verses 7–11 He complains of the mockery of His enemies and God's failure to answer Him.

Verses 12–21 consist of four stanzas. The first three describe what Jesus' enemies were doing to Him. Verses 12–13 compare His enemies to bulls and a lion surrounding Him and gaping on Him with their mouths. In verses 14–15, He complains about the physical results of His enemies' attack. In verses 16–18, He compares His enemies to dogs and cries out about the humiliations they are inflicting on Him. Verses 19–21 contain the final petition for deliverance.

In the second part of the psalm (vv. 22–31), the psalmist celebrates His deliverance. He will proclaim what God has done in the congregation and call the congregants to join Him in praise (vv. 22–26). All nations will hear and worship (vv. 27–29). The joyful news will be passed on to generations to come (vv. 30–31).

The transition between parts one and two is very abrupt.

Save me from the mouth of the lion
And from the horns of the wild oxen!
You have answered me.
I will declare Your name to My brothers.

But this is exactly what happened to our Lord Jesus Christ at the moment of His death. He cried, "Father, into Your hands I commit my spirit." He died, and His soul was immediately in His Father's presence. A little while later, the same instantaneous transformation from suffering to glory happened for the thief to whom Jesus had said, "Today you will be with me in Paradise."

Pay special attention now to the first part of the psalm. It reveals many details of the crucifixion, almost to the point that it is a description of the scene. It is also a prayer of Jesus, so we have here His own perspective on His suffering as He cried to His Father for deliverance.

The first circumstance related to the cross is the cry of desolation in verse 1. Jesus' greatest pain was that God had forsaken Him (cf. Matt. 27:46). All the other circumstances are evidence of it. His God, whom He loved and longed for with all His heart, to whom He had been obedient all His life, and to whom He was still obedient, had left Him without help or comfort.

There are other specific references to the scene at the cross. The chief priests, scribes, and elders mocked Jesus with words very similar to verses 6–8 (cf. Matt. 27:43). They knew precisely what they were doing. They knew that Psalm 22 is a prophetic messianic psalm. They knew that verses 6–8 were somehow words that pertained to the Messiah. They were throwing in Jesus' face His messianic claim by mocking Him with those mocking words.

Verses 12–13 are a metaphorical description of proud and powerful enemies. At the cross were leaders of the Jews, soldiers of Rome, and ordinary people. Behind the cross was the authority of Pontius Pilate, the representative of Rome. Herod had played his own part in the infamous trials.

Verse 15 describes His thirst (cf. Jn. 19:28).

Verse 16 says, "They pierced my hands and my feet." The meaning of the Hebrew word translated here as *pierced* is in doubt. Some think it should be *bound.* Some think the line means, "Like a lion they enclosed [or surrounded] my hands and my feet." Still others think the word should be *shamed.* None of those suggestions sound convincing, but there is enough doubt about it that we cannot be certain that the verse is a reference to the piercing of Jesus' hands and feet with the nails of the crucifixion. However, all the major English translations use the word *pierced.*

Verse 17 says, "I can count all my bones. They look and

stare at me." There were people at the cross who seem to have been interested only in the spectacle (Luke 23:35). But their mere standing to gaze was humiliating to Jesus because of His nakedness.

Verse 18 carries this notion of nakedness further. The Gospels recount a very precise fulfillment of it. We would probably never guess that the psalmist is talking about different treatment for the different pieces of his clothing, but that is what happened.

> *Then the soldiers, when they had crucified Jesus, took His garments and made four parts, to every soldier a part, and His tunic; but the tunic was seamless, woven from the top throughout. Therefore they said among themselves, "Let us not tear it up, but cast lots for it, whose it will be:" that the scripture might be fulfilled, which says, "They divided My garments among them, and for My clothing they cast the lot." Therefore, these things the soldiers did.*
>
> —John 19:23–24

There are three other complaints in Psalm 22 that may also refer to specific circumstances of the crucifixion. Verse 2 says He cried day and night. This may be a reference both to Jesus' prayers in Gethsemane and His prayers from the cross. In verse 14, the sufferer says, "All my bones are out of joint." Is this perhaps a reference to the extreme pressure of the weight of His body on the joints of His arms, shoulders, and back? And verse 17 says,

"I can count all my bones." Does this mean that as Jesus' head hung down over His tortured body, He could see His bones standing out against His stretched flesh? It is at least a possibility.

There is one more thing to notice about the first eleven verses. The word *but* occurs at least four times.

O my God, I cry by day, and You do not answer,
And by night, and there is no silence for me,
But You are holy.

He cried, but He received no answer. He received no answer but remained convinced that God is holy.

In You our fathers trusted.
They trusted, and You delivered them.
To You they cried and were rescued.
They trusted and were not ashamed.
But I am a worm and not a man.

The knowledge that God delivered the fathers contrasted sharply with His own lack of an answer and added greatly to His distress.

In verse 9, after citing the mocking words of His enemies, Jesus says, "But You are He who drew me forth from the womb." He reminds Himself of the years from His conception to the present. Then God had been His God, but now God is far away. The remembrance of past mercies makes present desolation harder to bear.

These contrasts show how He was torn back and forth: "I cry, but You . . . Our fathers trusted, but I . . . My enemies mock, but You . . . "

Conclusion

Some psalms speak in a more general way of our Lord's suffering. Others are very specific. Psalm 22 is the most specific of all. We can almost say that it lays out for us the scene at Golgotha as our Lord Himself experienced it from the cross. The psalm is, in fact, so specific that we cannot understand it except as it was fulfilled at the cross. David was probably quite at a loss to understand his own words.

But the psalm is also a prayer, the crying out of our Lord to His God in the desolation of His soul, the pangs of His body, and the humiliation of His circumstances as He took the burden of our judgment on Himself.

We should always sing the first part of this psalm as a reminder of what Jesus suffered for us, especially in His being forsaken by God. And the second part is a reminder that He has passed from suffering to glory to help us endure the suffering of our own lives until we inherit the glory He is preparing for us.

Chapter 7
DEATH AND BURIAL

Christ's death and burial are inseparable, especially as they appear in the Book of Psalms. This chapter, therefore, considers them together.

Christ's Death

The Book of Psalms talks a lot about death. Approximately thirty-five psalms mention the word *death* and its cognates, and others use words closely associated with death such as *pit*, *grave*, *corruption*, and *body* (in the sense of dead body).

Though this may seem to be a morbid preoccupation with death, it is reasonable because of the circumstances of God's people in the world. First, the scriptural concept of death is much broader than physical death. Death came into the world because of sin and the judgment of God. Besides physical death, it includes spiritual death (being dead in trespasses and sins) and eternal death in hell. The Book of Psalms includes all three of these things in the concept of death. Sometimes only physical death is in view (Ps. 48:14), but at other times the psalmists are very much aware of death as judgment. In Psalm 49:14, it is the end of those who trust in riches, and the grave is the place where death shepherds them. It is being cut off from the land of the living (Ps. 52:5) and the light of the living (Ps. 56:13). There is no remembrance of God there or giving thanks to Him (Ps. 6:5). It is a thing of terror (Ps. 55:4). The grave, the pit, corruption, and darkness are its associates.

Second, the intense focus of the Book of Psalms on the antithesis (the enmity between the seed of the woman and the seed of the serpent) means death played a large role in the psalmists' thinking. They often felt seriously threatened by their enemies. They wrote their songs in the midst of war and conflict. Because our wars are not usually waged with physical weapons, we do not as frequently feel the threat of physical death. Nevertheless, we battle the spiritual hosts of wickedness in heavenly places, and separating us from God (which is death) is their goal. Perhaps we ought to feel more threatened than we do.

Though there are exceptions (especially Ps. 16), death in the Book of Psalms is usually not the gateway to heaven that our Lord Jesus Christ has made it for us. Rather, it is the result of the murderous hatred of enemies and being cut off from God. That, after all, is the purpose of our enemies: to destroy hope, deprive of comfort, and entice from the path of life so the righteous may perish with them in everlasting darkness.

Psalm 18 is a prophetic messianic psalm (see vv. 48–50). It is not only about David's deliverance from his enemies but also about the victories of our Lord Jesus Christ. The threat of death is the first trouble that David (and our Lord) address in this psalm.

The pangs of death encompass me,
And the torrents of belial dismayed me.
The pangs of sheol surround me.
The snares of death meet me.

—Ps. 18:4–5

Psalm 22 begins with death (forsakenness) and only moves to life in verses 21–22. The same thing happens in Psalm 9:13–14.

Be gracious to me, O Yahweh!
See my affliction from those who hate me,
You who exalt me from the gates of death,
That I may recount all Your praises
In the gates of the daughter of Zion.

By his betrayal, Judas fulfilled Psalm 55:13. In verses 4–5 of the same psalm, our Lord describes His terror of death.

My heart writhed in my inward parts,
And terrors of death fall on me.
Fear and trembling came into me,
And shuddering covered me.

This is not fear of physical death but dread of the absolute forsakenness of the cross: "My God, my God!" With that fear consuming Him, Jesus sweated blood in the Garden of Gethsemane.

Psalm 89 is another prophetic messianic psalm, and the last part of it is about the suffering of the anointed king. "What mighty man will live and not see death? Will he make his soul slip away from the hand of sheol?" (v. 48). This question arises because Yahweh has renounced the unbreakable covenant and cast His crown to the ground. The king asks, "How long, Yahweh? Will You hide to perpetuity? Will Your indignation burn like fire?" (v. 46). And he ends his song with a petition.

Remember, Lord, the reproach of Your servants.
I bear in my bosom the reproach of all the many peoples,
With which Your enemies reproach, O Yahweh,
With which they reproach the footsteps of Your anointed.

All these psalms and many more that are not so obviously messianic speak of the death of Christ.

Christ's Burial

The Hebrew language uses a number of words for the grave or hell. The main one is *sheol,* usually translated in the King James Version as "the grave" or "hell." Many explain the word in the same way the New International Version translates it: "realm of the dead." But this translation is too much under the influence of pagan mythology. Because contemporary English speakers are usually familiar with the word *sheol,* a transliteration rather than a translation is best. But the word has very negative connotations throughout Scripture. The psalmists often pray to be delivered from sheol. The King James Version communicates the correct idea. Sheol is the grave seen as the doorway to hell. Its most common synonyms are "the pit" (the hole in the ground in which our bodies are buried and return to dust under the judgment of God), "corruption," and "darkness." Two or more of these four words often appear together in parallelisms.

Some psalms mention the burial of Jesus in a rather passing way. We have already referred to Psalm 18:4–5 for death, but it also mentions sheol: "The pangs of sheol surrounded me." Psalm 30 is a psalm of thanksgiving by David at the dedication of his house. The Lord had established him in his kingdom (2 Sam. 5:11–12) and delivered him from Saul and his supporters.

O Yahweh, You have brought up from sheol my soul.
You have made me live instead of descending to the pit.

What profit is there in my blood,
When I go down to destruction?
Will the dust give thanks to You?
Will it declare Your truth?

—Ps. 30:3, 9

Psalm 40:2 should be interpreted in light of the clearly messianic verses 6–8 (cf. Heb. 10:5–10): "And He brought me up from the pit of tumult, From the miry mud." It too is about the burial of Christ and His rescue from it. Psalm 69:15 suggests that the psalmist is already in the pit but that it has not yet been closed over him: "And do not let the pit shut over me its mouth." Psalm 86 is a psalm of thanksgiving. In verse 13, David says, "You have rescued my soul from lowest sheol."

All these are more or less passing references to sheol and the pit. There are especially three psalms that talk about the burial of the Lord Jesus in a more detailed way. Psalm 16 is more about the resurrection than the burial of Christ, but verses 9–10 are important because in them our Lord confesses His own understanding of His burial. "My flesh will abide in hope. For You will not abandon My soul to sheol, Neither will You give Your Holy One to see corruption." He knew that He would not be in the grave long enough to return to dust. He spent only three days there before God raised him from the dead.

Psalm 88 is another psalm about death and sheol. Its great sorrow is unrelieved by any deliverance or turning to hope. The psalmist has not lost his faith—he continues to seek God—but he is otherwise in great trouble. Death, sheol, and the pit are very much on his mind. Verses 3–7 mention sheol, the pit, the dead, the slain, sheol again, the lowest pit, darkness, the depths, and all God's waves. He is like the dead whom God has forgotten, who are cut off from His hand, and upon whom God's wrath lies heavily. Verses 10–12 say of the dead that for them God will work no wonders.

Will Your lovingkindness be recounted in the tomb,
Your faithfulness in Abaddon?
Will Your wonders be known in the dark,
And Your righteousness in the land of forgetfulness?

Verses 14–17 add to the picture. God has cast off His soul and hidden His face. He is ready to die, suffering terrors and distraught. God's fierce wrath has overwhelmed Him.

This is our Lord in the Garden of Gethsemane crying, "If it be possible, let this cup pass from Me." And on the cross, "My God, My God, why have You forsaken me?"

The servant of the Lord is a title for Jesus in Isaiah. Psalm 143 is a "servant psalm," along with Psalms 89 and 119. "Do not enter into judgment with Your servant" (v. 2), and "Cause all those who distress my soul to perish, because I am Your servant" (v. 12). David, foreshadowing the suffering of Christ, says of his enemy, "He has crushed my life to the earth, He has made me dwell in darkness like those dead from antiquity" (v. 3). "Do not hide Your face from me, or I will be like those who descend to the pit" (v. 7).

Conclusion

In these psalms we see our Lord Jesus Christ bearing for us the final parts of the burden of God's wrath, even descending to death and sheol. Jesus left undone nothing that was necessary for our salvation. He took on Himself and to the end every part of the judgment of God against us. Thus He delivered us from the power of sheol. Our flesh will rest in hope. We will walk before the Lord in the land of the living.

Chapter 8
EXALTATION

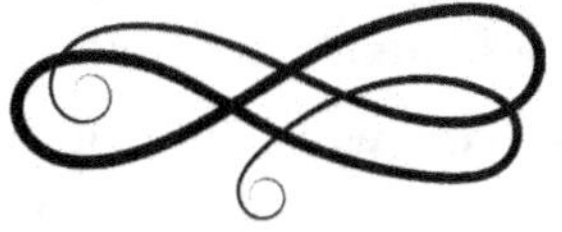

Our Lord's exaltation consists of four steps: resurrection, ascension to heaven, sitting at the right hand of the Father, and returning for judgment.

The Book of Psalms has much to say about all of these, though especially the last two. Most of the psalms come from the time of David and the establishment of the kingdom. It is not surprising that they have much to say about the kingdom and its king. But this should also be true of a New Testament perspective. We and all nations live under the reign of the exalted Christ, and He is even now extending and establishing His kingdom through the preaching of the gospel.

Resurrection

Psalm 30:3, 56:13, and 86:13, already considered in connection with the death and burial of Christ, are also relevant to the resurrection, especially when they mention deliverance from sheol. There is no need to say anything more about them.

There are several psalms to mention in passing before looking in more detail at others.

Psalm 71:20–21: "You, who have made me see many and evil troubles, Will make me live again, And from the depths of the earth You will bring me up again." There is nothing explicitly messianic about this psalm. Yet because of the fellowship of suffering between our Lord and ourselves, the psalmist's suffering at the hands of wicked men was a partaking of the suffering of Christ. The Lord brought up Christ again from the depths of earth.

In Psalm 91:14–16, the Most High promises to deliver, set on high, answer, and honor the One who sets his love on Him. "With length of days I will satisfy him and cause him to see my salvation." The Son set His love on the Father and did His will. All His life the Father was with Him, and at the end, the Father satisfied the Son with everlasting life.

Psalm 142 is a prayer of David, an Old Testament anointed one, for deliverance from enemies who secretly set a snare for him. David's son, the Messiah whom David foreshadowed, also prayed:

Cause my soul to come forth from the dungeon
That I may give thanks to Your name.
The righteous will surround me
For You will reward me.

God answered His prayer. Jesus came forth from sheol and is even now surrounded by all the righteous who have followed Him from death to life.

Four psalms require a more detailed look. Psalm 2 is rich in its Christology; previous chapters pointed out its connection with Christ's anointing, incarnation, and resurrection. These three things come together in His kingship. God anointed Jesus to be King, He was born King, and He rose from the dead to be seated at God's right hand. In fact, all the aspects of His exaltation center on His royal power, and even His humiliation was the way to it. He became man and died so He might become universal King. "He humbled Himself. . . . Therefore God also has highly exalted Him" (Phil. 2:8–9).

Describing the resurrection as a begetting (Ps. 2:7) is simply an extension of other scriptural teaching. In Colossians 1:18, Paul calls Christ the firstborn from the dead. John does the same thing in Revelation 1:5. The scriptures tie resurrection to begetting also in regeneration; God has begotten us again to a living hope (1 Pet. 1:3). This is the same thing as being raised with Christ (Col. 3:1). Therefore, according to Psalm 2, Christ was begotten or raised to inherit the nations.

Psalm 16 is a pilgrim's song. It begins with a prayer that is always appropriate to those who are living in a hostile foreign country: "Preserve me, O God." In the second part (vv. 2–6), David remembers that even as a pilgrim he had a wonderful portion here in this life: "Yahweh is the portion of my share and my cup." In verse 7 he blesses the Lord for counsel. Believers face many difficult problems and questions in the course of their pilgrimage, but they always have the Word of God for guidance.

Verses 8–11 are especially about Jesus. They show us a progression in His relation to the Lord. In verse 8, He sets the Lord before Him. The Lord is first His goal, the end of His pilgrim journey. Then the Lord is at His right hand to guide, protect, and advise Him while He travels. After death, His flesh rests hopefully in sheol. After death (v. 11), having reached the end of his journey, He stands in the presence of the Lord. And in the final line of the psalm, He stands at the Lord's right hand. The psalm moves from earth to heaven, from the journey to its goal, from suffering to glory, traveling and ending in the presence of the Lord. The Lord was both before Him and at His right hand during His pilgrimage. He will stand before the Lord and at His right hand in glory.

Peter said of these words:

> *David . . . died and was buried, and his sepulcher is among us until this day. [He] having foreseen, spoke concerning the resurrection of Christ, that His soul was not left in Hades, nor did His flesh see corruption. This Jesus God raised up.*
>
> —Acts 2:29–32

Both Peter and Paul saw in the psalm a prophecy of the resurrection of Christ and specifically exclude David and others from it. After explaining that the resurrection fulfilled Psalm 2 and Isaiah 55, Paul continues:

> *Because of this He says also in another psalm: "You will not give Your Holy One to see corruption." For David, after he had rendered service to his own generation by the purpose of God, fell asleep and was gathered with his fathers and saw corruption; but He whom God raised did not see corruption.*
>
> —Acts 13:35–37

Psalm 116 is a psalm about deliverance from death. There are two stanzas in it that at least imply the resurrection. The first is verses 5–9. Verse 6 refers to Christ's low estate and verse 7 to His return to rest. God makes rest perfect in the land of rest (heaven). Christ then gives thanks in verses 8–9: "You have rescued my soul from death . . . I will walk before the face of Yahweh in the land of the living." The second is verses 15–19. The stanza begins, "Precious in the eyes of Yahweh is the death of His saints." Our Lord then confesses to Yahweh the truth of this, learned from His own experience. "I am Your servant, the son of Your maidservant. You have loosened my bonds." That is cause for thanksgiving (v. 17), which He will offer in the "presence of all His people, in the courts of the house of Yahweh, in your midst, O Jerusalem" (vv. 18–19). The spiritual house of Yahweh is the church in the New Testament, which will be made perfect in heaven. Christ has passed from death to everlasting life.

Psalm 118 is perhaps more about the ascension or the sitting at God's right hand than resurrection, but it fits here too because it is another psalm about deliverance from the troubles of this life. "All nations surrounded me. . . . They surrounded me; yes, they surrounded me. . . . They surrounded me like bees" (vv. 10–12). But the Lord helped Him and did not give Him over to death. Therefore, He enters the gates of righteousness. He calls on them to open to Him so He may enter and praise the Lord. He is the "stone which the builders rejected" (1 Pet. 2:7), but God has exalted Him to the head of the corner. His people receive Him as He comes: "Blessed is he who comes in the name of Yahweh! We bless you from the house of Yahweh" (v. 26). These are the words the people sang at our Lord's triumphal entry (Matt. 21:9). Having entered the gates, He offers thanks.

> *Yahweh is God,*
> *And He has given light to us.*
> *Bind the festal sacrifice with cords to the horns of the altar.*
> *You are my God, and I will give thanks to You.*
> *My God, I will exalt You.*
>
> —Ps. 118: 27–28

The psalm has a double fulfillment. When Christ rode triumphantly into Jerusalem, He entered the gates of righteousness, and the people received Him with hosannas. But this was only a foreshadowing of a greater triumph. It came just a few days later when He rose from the dead and entered the heavenly sanctuary.

Ascension

Because our Lord's exaltation was from the earthly realm to the heavenly and from death to life, the psalms discussed in previous chapters come up again. Christ was made a little lower than the angels and then crowned with glory and honor (Ps. 8).

> *It was fitting for Him, because of whom are all things and through whom are all things, while leading many sons to glory, to perfect the captain of their salvation through sufferings. For both He who sanctifies and those who are being sanctified are all from one.*
>
> —Heb. 2:10–11

Psalm 57 is also a psalm of humiliation, but it anticipates glory: "Be exalted above the heavens, O God. Above all the earth be your glory" (vv. 5, 11). Psalm 91:14–16 not only promises long life but also a setting on high and honor.

There are, however, at least three psalms that are very explicit about the ascension. Psalm 24:3 is similar to Psalm 15:1. The difference between the two is that Psalm 15 uses the words *abide* and *dwell*, while Psalm 24 uses the words *ascend* and *stand*. "Who may ascend into the hill of Yahweh?" Verses 4–6 answer the question: "He who has clean hands and a pure heart." That applies to us only as we are in Christ, but He is the undefiled High Priest who offered Himself for the sins of the people (Heb. 7:27) and then ascended into heaven.

Verses 7–10 describe His ascension from the perspective of observers.

Lift up, O gates, your heads,
And be lifted up, O everlasting doors,
And the king of glory shall come in!
Who is this king of glory?
Yahweh, strong and mighty,
Yahweh, mighty in battle!
Lift up, O gates, your heads!
And be lifted up, O everlasting doors,
And the king of glory shall come in!
Who is He, this king of glory?
Yahweh of hosts,
He is the king of glory!

It is possible that David composed this psalm to celebrate the bringing of the ark of the covenant to Jerusalem (2 Sam. 6), but there can be no question that its fulfillment is in the ascension of Christ. Therefore, "The earth belongs to Yahweh, and its fullness, The world and those who dwell in it. For He founds it on the seas And establishes it on the floods" (Ps. 24:1–2).

Psalm 47 is a celebration of the triumph of Yahweh over the nations. "He is a great king over all the earth. He subdued the peoples under us, and the nations under our feet" (vv. 2–3).

How has He accomplished it? "God has ascended with a shout, Yahweh with the sound of a ram's horn. . . . God reigns over the nations. God sits on His holy throne" (vv. 5, 8). His Son has ascended into heaven to sit at His right hand. The princes of the earth will become the people of the God of Abraham (v. 9).

All of Psalm 68 is about the ascension and power of Christ, but there is not time and space here to discuss the whole of it. Probably it also began as a celebration of the ark's return to Jerusalem. The words of verse 1 are the words the priests cried as the ark went forth before God's people in the wilderness (Num. 10:35): "Let God rise up. Let His enemies be scattered, and let those who hate Him flee from before His face!" God was going before His army to lead them to victory in the Promised Land.

Paul interpreted verse 18 in Ephesians 4:8–10.

> *Having ascended into the height, He took captivity captive and gave gifts to men. (But this, "He ascended"—what is it except that He also descended first into the lower parts of the earth? The one who descended, He is also the one who ascended far above all the heavens, so that He might fill all things.*

The verses following describe the gifts Jesus gave to His people following His ascension.

Verses 24–27 describe the procession of His people with Him into heaven.

They have seen Your processions, O God,
The processions of my God, my King, into the sanctuary . . .
There is little Benjamin their ruler;
The princes of Judah, their council;
The princes of Zebulun; the princes of Naphtali.

Those are two southern tribes and two northern tribes. They represent all the people of God.

And the nations also come.

Because of Your temple at Jerusalem,
To You kings will carry presents.
Rebuke the beasts of the reeds...
Until everyone submits himself with pieces of silver...
Envoys will come out of Egypt;
Ethiopia will quickly stretch out her hands to God.
—Ps. 68:29–31

These three psalms, connected with their Old Testament references and New Testament interpretations, bring together four things: the procession of the ark before Israel in the wilderness, the return of the ark to Jerusalem, the triumphal entry, and our Lord's ascension into heaven. The ascension is the culmination and fulfillment of all of them.

Sitting at the Right Hand of God

The exaltation of Jesus to the right hand of His Father was, of course, His crowning as King of the universe. It is also the continuation of His work as our High Priest since it is from there that He makes intercession for us (Rom. 8:34). The chapter on Christ's anointing covered His kingship, so this chapter will focus on what the psalms say about his work as King.

There are two series of psalms in the Psalter about the reign of Christ. All of them reveal him to us as Yahweh, the God of Israel.

The first series is Psalms 93–99. Three of these begin with the declaration, "Yahweh reigns!" Believers today say, "Jesus is Lord." Psalm 93 is about His reign over the seas: "Mightier than the sound of many waters, Mightier than the breakers of the sea, Mighty on high is Yahweh!" Jesus fulfilled this psalm in part when He calmed the storm on the Sea of Galilee. Psalm 97 is about His righteousness: "Righteousness and justice are the foundation of his throne" (v. 2). He fulfilled this by the shedding of His blood. It laid the foundation for His own triumph over darkness and our salvation from sin and death in the righteousness of God. Psalm 99 emphasizes His holiness (vv. 3, 5, 9), as well as His justice: "And the strength of the king loves justice. You establish uprightness, justice and righteousness in Jacob" (v. 4).

All the other psalms in the series are also about His reign. In Psalm 94 He is the God of vengeance on the wicked: "O God of vengeance, shine forth!" Psalm 95 summons us to worship Him because He is the great God over all gods and the earth (v. 3) and also because He is our God (v. 7). Psalm 96 calls us to declare His glory among the nations because He is greater than all gods, reveals Himself in His sanctuary, and is coming for judgment. Psalm 98 exhorts us to sing and "shout joyfully before the king, Yahweh" (v. 6).

The second series is Psalms 144–150. In Psalm 144 David and his Son praise Yahweh because "He subdues my people under me" (v. 2), delivers from foreigners, and blesses His people. Psalm 145 extols the glory of Yahweh's kingdom (vv. 11–13). Psalm 146 recounts His blessings to His people and concludes, "Yahweh shall reign forever, Your God, O Zion, to generation after generation." Psalm 147 praises Yahweh for His blessings to His people (vv. 4–6, 19–20) and His care for the rest of His creation (vv. 7–18). Psalm 148 is a command to all creatures in heaven and on earth to praise Yahweh. "His name alone is high, His splendor is over earth and heaven," and "He has exalted the horn of His people." Psalm 149 urges the children of Zion to be joyful in their King because He has appointed them to execute vengeance on the nations. They do it with the two-edged sword of His Word. Psalm 150 is a summons to everything that has breath (v. 6) to praise Yahweh in the sanctuary (v. 1) for His mighty acts (v. 2), with all kinds of musical instruments (vv. 3–5). In all of these, Jesus is Yahweh the King.

In addition to these two series, three psalms lay the foundation for our understanding of Christ's royal power. In Psalm 110, Yahweh commands David's Lord to sit down at His right hand. Psalms 89 and 132 describe His covenant with David and David's Son who will sit on His throne forever. The foundation is God's eternal purpose and His promise to David.

There are other psalms that talk particularly about Christ's kingly work. Psalm 21 is about Yahweh's blessings to the King whom He has crowned, to whom He has given everlasting life, and through whom He devours His enemies. Psalm 22, the first part of which describes the crucifixion, concludes with prophecy about Christ's rule over the nations (vv. 27–29) and to all generations (vv. 30–31).

In Psalm 45, the psalmist addresses the king and queen at their wedding. He urges both to fulfill their royal and conjugal duties. The king must gird his sword to ride out against enemies, love righteousness and hate wickedness, and receive the queen at his right hand (vv. 2–9). The queen must forget her people and her father's house and present herself to the king (vv. 10–15). Together they will bear sons who will become princes in all the earth (v. 16). The sons are the children of God (cf. Ezek. 16:20–21) born again through Christ and His bride. The New Testament parallels are found in Ephesians 5:32 and Revelation 19:6–16, 21–22.

The Psalter has only two of Solomon's 1,005 songs (cf. 1 Kings 4:32). They are Psalms 127 and 72. Psalm 127 is not relevant here, but Psalm 72 is a recounting of the blessings of Messiah's reign. He will bring justice (vv. 1–7), have universal dominion (vv. 8–15), establish great prosperity (v. 16) and reign forever (v. 17).

Finally, Psalm 104 reveals the King's power in creation and His providential provision for His creatures.

These psalms therefore paint for us a detailed picture of

the reign of our Lord Jesus Christ over the church and the world.

Judgment

Judgment is one of the king's functions, but there is so much about this in the Book of Psalms that it is better to treat it separately.

Judgment is for both the righteous and the wicked. It destroys the wicked but purifies the righteous. David prays in Psalm 17, "From Your presence let my judgment come forth," and in Psalm 26, "Judge me, O Yahweh, For in my integrity I have walked." We can pray thus because our judge is also our Savior. But David also prays against his enemies: "Confront him, cast him down" (Ps. 17:13). Many other psalms threaten worse on the wicked.

Judgment is both temporal and eternal. Psalms 96 and 98 anticipate the Lord's coming for judgment at the end of time. When Old Testament believers sang these psalms, they were praying for the coming of the Messiah. He has come, but we continue to pray for the same thing with our hope set on His return. But Psalms 78 and 106 recount temporal judgments on Israel and are warnings to us that we too may fall under temporal judgments if we are faithless.

The Father has committed all judgment to the Son (John 5:22). When the psalms talk about judgment, that judgment comes from Him who has been appointed heir of the nations. He will deliver the righteous but will break the rebellious kings and rulers of earth in pieces like a potter's vessel.

In Psalm 9:7, God tells us that He is preparing His throne for judgment. That preparation took place in the exaltation of Jesus to God's own right hand.

In Psalm 75, God warns the wicked of coming judgment. "When I choose the appointed time, I will judge uprightly . . . God is the judge: This one He will humble And that one He will exalt." God has appointed the time of Christ's judgment. Then the wicked will drink the dregs of the cup of wrath prepared for them.

Psalm 76 is also about judgment, but especially about judgment on the wicked. That judgment will be for the deliverance of the oppressed of earth. God is known in Judah because there He broke the arrows of the bow, the shield, and the sword of battle. Our Lord works the salvation of His church through judgment on her enemies.

God declares His displeasure with the judges of the earth in Psalms 58 and 82. "Will you judge in uprightness, O sons of man? Truly in heart you work injustice." And God "among the gods will judge. How long will you judge unjustly, And lift up the faces of the wicked?" His judgment falls through the judgment by Christ Jesus.

Psalm 101 is a psalm of judgment on the church. "Early will I exterminate all the wicked of the land, To cut off from the city of Yahweh all the workers of iniquity." Judgment begins at the house of God (1 Pet. 4:17). Christ came to purge His threshing floor (Matt. 3:12).

In Psalm 50, the mighty God summons all His people to come before Him:

Gather to Me my saints,
Those who have cut a covenant with Me by sacrifice . . .
I will not receive a bull from your house . . .
Offer to God thanksgiving,
And pay your vows to the Most High.
But to the wicked God says,
What right do you have to declare My statutes
And to take up My covenant in your mouth?
—Ps. 50:5, 9, 14, 16

Psalm 62:12 declares that the Lord will reward everyone according to his works. It is the very same thing that Paul says of Christ in 2 Corinthians 5:10.

Psalm 67 is a prophecy of the harvest of the Gentiles in the New Testament. "The earth will yield its increase." It will happen because He "will judge the peoples with uprightness And lead the nations on the earth" (v. 4).

These psalms reveal all the aspects of Christ's judgment.

Conclusion

The glory of the Lord revealed in the face of Christ is a very prominent theme in the psalms. They are about His kingship and kingdom more than they are about anything else. They teach in great detail about the sufferings our King endured to obtain His throne, about His universal rule, and about all He will do to establish the everlasting kingdom of God.

Just as there is a fellowship of suffering between ourselves and Christ, so also is there a fellowship of glory. We are His children, "and if children, then heirs—heirs of God and co-heirs with Christ, if indeed we suffer with him, that we may also be glorified together" (Rom. 8:17). He has "made us to our God kings and priests, and we will reign upon the earth" (Rev. 5:10). This is another way we celebrate the God of our salvation in the psalms. Glory to Him!

Chapter 9

FULFILLMENT OF THE TYPES

The Scriptures are full of metaphorical or figurative language, but types or shadows (cf. Heb. 10:1) are a very special class among them. They are Old Testament institutions, persons, or ceremonies appointed by God to be prophetic symbols of New Testament realities (also called antitypes). Because types are prophetic and unknown apart from revelation, only God can establish them. Thus, Scripture teaches that David, the ceremonial cleansings, and the temple are types, but Judah pleading for Benjamin (Gen. 44) is not. God did not appoint Judah to that role. Judah's example illustrates intercession, but he is not a shadow or type of Christ in the formal sense.

Understanding all the types is important to understanding the Book of Psalms, so this chapter covers both types of Christ and types of other New Testament realities.

Types Not Directly Related to Christ

In the Book of Psalms there are many types of New Testament things other than Christ Himself. Israel's organization as a nation foreshadowed spiritual truths about the church. For example, the church is a people united and organized under a King and governed by the King's law. More than that, Israel was the church of the Old Testament. In Acts 7:38, the martyr Stephen said of Moses, "This is he who was in the church in the wilderness." The Greek word is *ekklesia*, the word that almost everywhere else in the New Testament is a name for the church. The main difference between the Old and New Testaments is that in the New Testament, God added the Gentiles to the Old Testament church (Eph. 2) and grafted them into the tree of the Jews (Rom. 11).

The psalmists used a variety of names for Israel. "Jacob" is a name that emphasizes especially that Israel is the chosen people. "Judah" recognizes the chief tribe, the tribe from which David and his line came. "People" (singular) separates Israel from "peoples" (plural). Almost always in the psalms, "people" means Israel, and "peoples" means the rest of the nations. Our translations, however, do not always pay attention to this distinction. Congregation and assembly are close synonyms and indicate that the people of God are one people gathered in the presence of God. Various metaphors such as vine (Ps. 80) and sheep or flock (Ps. 77 and 100) teach us specific things about their relation to God.

Because Israel itself was a type, much of its history, described in some detail in Psalms 78, 105, and 106, was also typical. The bondage in Egypt (cf. Ps. 80, 105, and others) is typical of bondage in sin. The introduction to the law— "I am the Lord your God who brought you out of the land of Egypt, out of the house of bondage"—is about our spiritual deliverance in Christ. Paul says in 1 Corinthians 10:1–2 that Israel was baptized into Moses in the cloud and in the sea, an event mentioned in Psalm 136 and others. Israel's journey through the wilderness (Ps. 68) is typical of our sojourn in a spiritually dry and thirsty land. Canaan, or "the land" (mentioned in many psalms), is typical of heaven (Heb. 11:16). Israel's wars (Ps. 83) are typical of our spiritual warfare (2 Cor. 10). All of Israel's history reflects in a general way the history of the church in the New Testament.

Jerusalem, sometimes called the daughter of Jerusalem, is also a type of the church, whether the word refers to the city itself or the people who inhabited it. Various names for it are Zion (Ps. 48), City of God (Ps. 87), holy hill (Ps. 3), and Salem (Ps. 76). Things that belong to it are symbols of spiritual realities in the church. Gates and bars (Ps. 122:2, 147:13) stand for spiritual defenses, palaces (Ps. 48) for spiritual prosperity and strength, and streets (Ps. 144) for the concourse of God's people.

Israel and the land of the living (Ps. 27:13; 52:5; 116:9; 142:5) are other names for the land of Canaan. Inheritance, portion, or lot are closely associated. They apply to the land as a whole (Ps. 47:4; 79:1), to the people as God's inheritance (Ps. 33:12; 68:9), or to the portion of a person or family in the land (Ps. 16:5–6). God gave the land to His people and to each family among them a portion to be its own. It signified to them their part in the kingdom of God and among His people, so believers attached great importance to it. Naboth refused to sell "the inheritance of my fathers" (1 Kings 21:3) to Ahab.

Therefore, fields, houses, flocks, herds, and other possessions also had spiritual significance. This sheds light on the Old Testament emphasis on prosperity. To believers it was not important in itself but rather a part of the goodly inheritance or portion that God had given. To us in the New Testament, these earthly gifts have much less significance. God calls us to seek spiritual blessings in heavenly places (Eph. 1:3) and the promise that heaven, earth, and all things in them will belong to us. "All things are yours: whether Paul or Apollos, or Cephas, or the world or life or death, or things present or things to come—all are yours. And you are Christ's, and Christ is God's" (1 Cor. 3:21–23). When Psalm 37 promises that we will inherit the earth or the land (v. 9) it does not mean this earth or the earthly land of Canaan but the kingdom of heaven and the new heavens and new earth to which we as new creatures already belong.

The temple and tabernacle were also types of the church (Eph. 2:19–22). They have many names in the psalms: sanctuary, holy place, house of God, dwelling place, pavilion, secret place, and courts of the Lord. These names all describe the temple as the place of God's throne, His dwelling place among His people, the particular location where He both revealed His glory and hid it behind the veil. Various metaphors designate it also as our place: the shadow or covert of His wings (a reference to the cherubim on the mercy seat), refuge, shelter, hiding place, and presence of the Lord. The house of God was the spiritual center of the land, the special place where the people went to meet with their God. Of it Jesus said, "Destroy this temple and in three days I will raise it up."

All the furnishings of the tabernacle were also significant. The ark that contained the table of the law and had cherubim hovering over it was the throne of God (Ps. 99:1) to which the people came, by way of the priesthood and its ceremonies, to worship. The pillar of cloud or fire that rested on the tabernacle in the wilderness signified the presence of God who is a consuming fire (Heb. 12:28–29). The altars of burnt offering and incense were the places where the people brought all their offerings. Malachi 1:7 and Psalm 23:5 call the altar of burnt offering a table, the place where God and His people eat together in fellowship. The altar of incense was the place of prayer (Ps. 141:2; Rev. 8:1–5). The table of shewbread and the candlestick signified the presence of the people in God's house, and the priesthood signified the mediation of Christ our Savior and Intercessor. The synagogues, which had their beginnings at Mount Sinai (Lev. 23:3), were an extension of the worship at the temple, a place where the people could meet with God weekly instead of just during the three annual feasts in Jerusalem.

Psalm 68 mentions many of these types: the ark at least by implication (v. 1 compared with Num. 10:35), the habitation of God (v. 5), the people, the exodus (v. 7), God's provision for Israel in the wilderness (vv. 9–10), the hill of Zion (vv. 15–16), the holy place (vv. 17, 35), a procession into the sanctuary (v. 24), and the temple and Jerusalem (v. 29).

The psalms demand that we know the spiritual significance of the types. Therefore, we should be familiar with the last part of Exodus— it describes the tabernacle and its furnishings—and the book of Leviticus which gives detailed commandments for many of the ceremonies.

Types of Christ

There are also types of Christ in the Book of Psalms. Persons such as David, Solomon, Aaron, Moses, Melchizedek, and others were Old Testament messiahs or christs. In a limited way, they prefigured Christ and His work—David as man of war, Solomon as man of rest, Aaron as high priest, Moses as intercessor and prophet, and Melchizedek as the royal priest to whose order Christ belongs (Heb. 7). When a psalm heading ascribes a song to David or Solomon, the psalm may also be about Christ Himself.

There are other types as well. Psalm 78:23–25 and 81:16 mention the manna. Jesus taught in John 6 that the manna is a type of Himself as the bread from heaven that gives life to the world. Paul says of the manna and the water from the rock mentioned in Psalms 78:15–16 and 114:8 that they "all ate the same spiritual food, and all drank the same spiritual drink. For they drank of that spiritual Rock following them, and the Rock was Christ" (1 Cor. 10:3–4). David said, "Purge me with hyssop and I shall be clean" (Ps. 51:7). Hyssop was used in cleansing rituals to sprinkle blood and water on people and things. Though it does not itself signify Christ, it calls attention to Christ's cleansing work.

Sacrifices make many appearances in the Book of Psalms. There are two general words for them, one that refers especially to the bloody sacrifices and the other to the other gifts that the people brought: tithes, bread, grain, wine, and oil.

The psalms also use specific words for the different kinds of offerings. Burnt offerings (Ps. 20:3; 40:6; 50:8; 51:16, 19; 66:13, 15) were bloody offerings that pointed the people to the need for atonement for their sins. They also were offerings by which the people dedicated themselves and their possessions to God. Sin offerings (Ps. 40:6) were to be offered for sins committed in ignorance. The law did not require freewill offerings (Ps. 54:6, 110:3, 119:108); they were voluntary expressions of gratitude and payments of vows. Psalm 110 says, "Your people will be a free will offering In the day of Your power." In the day of Christ's exaltation, they will freely offer themselves to fight for His cause in the world. The trespass offering and the peace offering are absent.

The psalms also mention the sacrificial animals: bulls (Ps. 50:9; 51:19; 66:15; 69:31), goats (Ps. 50:9; 66:15), oxen (Ps. 69:31), and rams (Ps. 66:15). The blood of these was shed at the altar of burnt offering to foreshadow the death of Christ for sin.

The law, having a shadow of good things coming and not the image itself of the things, can never by these sacrifices that they offered continually year by year make those who approach perfect. It is impossible for the blood of bulls and goats to take away sin. We have been sanctified through the offering of the body of Jesus Christ once for all (Heb. 10:1, 4, 10).

Our Lord finished all the bloody sacrifices and ceremonies of the Old Testament. Nonetheless, Christians continue to offer sacrifices without blood when they present their bodies as living sacrifices (Rom. 12:1), give tithes and offerings, serve God and His people, and praise God. Hosea 14:2 even says, "We will offer the calves of our lips." All the psalms are offerings of thanks to the God of our salvation, and they prophesy that the nations will bring such offerings.

The kings of Tarshish and of the isles will bring presents;
The king of Sheba and Seba will offer gifts.
Yes, all kings will fall down before Him;
All nations will serve Him.

—Ps. 72:10–11

The psalms use the metaphorical language of the Old Testament ceremonies to shed light on Christ Himself, Christian life and worship.

Conclusion

The Book of Psalms often makes use of typical and ceremonial language. Our Lord is He of whom they spoke. They are promise; He is fulfillment. They are prophecy; He is the Word spoken. They are types; He is the antitype. They are shadows; He is the reality that casts the shadow.

The Book of Psalms is filled with Christ. Dogmatics books sometimes divide the doctrine of Christ into four parts: His names, natures, offices, and states. We have spoken extensively about all of them as revealed in the psalms. The psalms speak of Him in different ways: by celebration of the God of our salvation, by prophecy in those psalms called messianic, by types and shadows, and by descriptions of His life and work in both suffering and glory. They even reveal far more of His words of prayer and praise than the gospels do. They are an exceedingly rich resource from which we can learn to know our God and Savior in all He is and all He has done for us. May God teach us to love them and celebrate by them the saving work of our Lord.

Appendix 1

SPEAKING TO ONE ANOTHER IN PSALMS

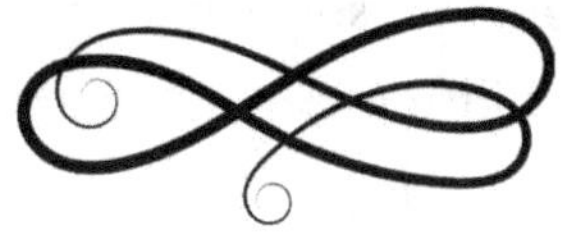

It may be helpful to our use of the psalms to point out some differences between Hebrew poetry and the kind of poetry hymns use. At least three things may be unexpected and confusing to Westerners whose ways of thinking and writing are different from those of the ancient Jews. They are (1) changes of grammatical person, (2) changes of speaker, and (3) changes of audience. These changes happen frequently and sometimes without warning.

Changes of Person, Speaker, and Audience

Changes of Person

Changes of person refers to grammatical person: first person, second person, and third person. First person uses the pronouns I, me, we, us, my, mine, and ours. Second person uses the pronouns you and your (the King James Version uses thee and thou for the singular forms). Third person uses the pronouns he, him, his, they, them, and their. The psalms frequently change person multiple times in twenty or thirty verses.

Psalm 27 is a simple example. In the first twelve verses, David speaks of himself in the first person singular: "Yahweh is my light and my salvation." But in the last two verses, he changes to second person singular: "Wait on Yahweh, be strong, and He will make your heart courageous." Since these verses use the singular rather than the plural, it is possible that David is talking to himself.

Psalm 44:8 gives us an example of something else that occurs frequently. In the lines preceding and following, the song addresses God directly (second person singular), but this stanza changes to third person.

You have saved us from our enemies,
And those who hate us You have put to shame.
In God [not in you] we boast all the day,
And to Your name forever we give thanks.

That is by no means all that happens in the psalm. There is an alternating back and forth between first person singular and first person plural. "We have heard" (v. 1). "You are my king" (v. 4). "Through You we will push down our enemies" (v. 5). "I will not trust in my bow" (v. 6). The sons of Korah, who wrote this psalm, may have had in mind one person who speaks the whole but sometimes speaks for himself and sometimes for the people of God. The obvious candidate for that role would be the king.

One more example will suffice, though there are many more. Psalm 34 begins with David speaking in the first person (vv. 1–2). Then he addresses others in the second person (v. 3). In verse 4 he switches back to the first person. In verse 5 he changes to the third person, talking about others. In verse 6 he talks again about himself, but this time in the third person singular ("This poor man cried"). Verse 7 is third person plural, and verse 8 is second person plural. This is an extreme example, but it shows that the composers of the psalms did not consider consistency of grammatical person to be as important as it is to modern English writers. If we are not prepared to accept this difference between ourselves and them, we will flounder.

Changes of Speaker

Speakers also change frequently. It's necessary to ask the question, "Who is talking?"

Psalm 2 has four parts. In the first three verses, the psalmist is talking, but at the end he quotes the words of the rebellious kings and rulers. The word *saying* that appears in our translations is not in the Hebrew. The speaker has changed, and we know it only because the psalmist would not say those words; they belong to someone else. The same thing happens in the second stanza (vv. 4–6). The psalmist is talking, but at the end he quotes the words of the Lord, again without inserting the word *saying*. In the third stanza, there is an entirely different speaker. It is not the psalmist or the kings or the Lord, but the Lord's Anointed. He says, "I will recount the decree," and goes on to quote the words of the Lord to him: "You are My Son." In the fourth stanza, the psalmist talks again, this time addressing the kings and judges of the earth. The material in these verses is his own words.

Psalm 4 may be another example. Though many commentators would not agree, verse 2 is clearer if understood as a word of God Himself: "How long will you turn My glory to shame?" But the verses before and after are David's words.

In Psalm 32, David begins with a confession of his personal experience of the truth of justification by faith. But in verses 8–9, without any indication except the words themselves, the Lord speaks: "I will instruct you." In verses 10–11, David speaks again.

Being aware of these changes of speaker will help to understand the psalms and may even stimulate some penetrating questions that would not otherwise have surfaced.

These changes of speaker raise another question. Why sing someone else's words? That question can be broken down into more specific questions. Why sing God's words? Why sing the words of Jesus? Why sing the words of other people?

If the words of God are addressed to us, we read and sing them to help them take root in our hearts and to let God know that we have heard Him and will obey. If the words of God are addressed to others, we sing them because God has commanded us to teach and admonish one another in psalms and hymns and spiritual songs, and because this is one way we fulfill our calling to witness to the world.

If the words are the words of Jesus, we sing them because we are one with Him. We sing Psalm 22 not only to remind ourselves what He has done for us but also because our old man has been crucified with Him (Rom. 6:6). Even though we know we will see corruption, we sing Psalm 16 with Him because we still have certainty that He will show us the path of life and we will join Him at God's right hand to enjoy everlasting pleasures. We sing His words of suffering because God has given to us the gift of partaking of His sufferings. We sing His words of exultation because we exult with Him in His glory and the glory He gives us.

Some psalms address others besides us. We join our voices to the God's audience to reinforce what He has said. They may also be addressed to us. We sing them to ourselves so we will not forget.

And in all this we remember that we are part of the great company in the heavenly Jerusalem, the host of angels, the church triumphant, the church militant, and Jesus the mediator of the new covenant shouting with joy to the God of our salvation and proclaiming His judgments in all the earth.

Changes of Audience

The third thing to see is that audiences within a psalm may also change. The psalms do not always speak directly to God, though He is, of course, always the primary audience and a listener to their words. One part of the psalm may be spoken to one person or group and another part to God or someone else.

In the first part of Psalm 55, David talks to God, but in verses 12–14 he talks to a friend who betrayed him. Verses 15–21 mention no audience; David may be meditating aloud. In verse 22 he uses the second person singular, so he is probably talking to himself. In verse 23 he talks again to God.

Psalm 68 has many changes of audience. The list includes at least the righteous (v. 4), God (v. 7), mountains (v. 16), God again (v. 18), ourselves (vv. 19–20), God again (v. 24), the people (v. 26), God again (v. 29), the kingdoms of the earth (v. 32), and God again (v. 35). In this case, David identifies each one as he begins to speak.

Psalm 137 has four parts (vv. 1–4, 5–6, 7, 8–9). In the first part, the people of God talk to each other. In the second they talk to Jerusalem, in the third to God, and in the fourth to the daughter of Babylon. The psalm carefully identifies each one.

To whom a psalm or part of a psalm is addressed is important.

Further Exploration of Audience

The subject of audience deserves further exploration.

In Colossians 3:16, the Apostle Paul exhorts the church, "Let the word of Christ dwell in you richly in all wisdom, teaching and admonishing one another in psalms and hymns and spiritual songs, singing with grace in your hearts to the Lord."[5] In the psalms we speak not only to each other as fellow saints but to many others as well—to our own souls, to enemies, to the whole world, to inanimate creatures, and to heaven and those who live there. The Lord wants the whole universe to hear His Word through the words and songs of His people.

There is some of this diversity of audience in hymnbooks: "O Come All Ye Faithful;" "O Day of Rest and Gladness;" "Come, Take by Faith the Body of the Lord;" "Soul, Adorn Yourself with Gladness;" "All Hail the Power of Jesus' Name;" "God Be with You Till We Meet Again;" "To God Be the Glory." But the psalms do it much more frequently and with much greater variety, both in the audiences addressed and the subjects broached.

The context of Colossians 3:16 is exhortation, and the nearer context is exhortation toward godly conduct in our fellowship with the saints. "Lie not to one another" (v. 9). "Put on tender mercies, kindness, humility, meekness, longsuffering, bearing with one another and forgiving one another" (vv. 12–13). "Put on love" (v. 14). "Let the peace of God rule in your hearts" (v. 15). And at the end of this series, "Let the word of Christ. . . ."

---

[5] Since the church at that time had very few or perhaps no songs besides the psalms, the three terms—psalms, hymns, and spiritual songs—are probably names that describe the psalms, but from different points of view.

The exhortation could mean to let the Word dwell in each one of you individually. Be storing it up in your minds so it may bear fruit in your lives. But it could also mean to let the Word dwell among you richly. Let it be present with the church, known and spoken by all, working and active among the members, bearing fruit for the good of all. The second seems preferable in the context of exhortations intended for the edification of the body. But both are necessary. The body will not be healthy if its members are sick. "If one member suffers all the members suffer with it" (1 Cor. 12:26).

The exhortation continues: "teaching and admonishing one another in psalms." The same is true in the parallel passage in Ephesians 5. The Apostle Paul urges the members of the church to be teaching and admonishing one another; that is a necessary part of the church's life and is not practiced enough today. But he recommends singing the psalms as the vehicle for this instruction and admonition.

That is very striking. Paul himself says that "every Scripture is profitable for teaching, for conviction, for correction, for training in righteousness" (2 Tim. 3:16), but here he calls attention especially to the psalms and the singing of them. We are to be teaching and admonishing one another in our songs. Attentive reading of the psalms will make it immediately obvious that the apostle had good reason to say it.

Sometimes we speak to ourselves. "Why are you cast down, O my soul? And why are you disquieted within me? Hope in God" (Ps. 42:5, 11; 43:5). In Psalm 57:8, David calls himself to praise, to wait on God (Ps. 62:5), and to return to His rest (Ps. 116:7). Almost all of Psalm 103 is a reminder to the singer of the many blessings God has given: "Bless the Lord, O my soul; And all that is within me, bless His holy name" (Ps. 103:1). It ends with a calling on the angels and the Lord's works to join the chorus. We should not forget that we are doing this publicly so others hear us and may join with us in doing the same thing.

It's not clear who the person addressed in Psalms 91 and 121 is. In both psalms, "you" is singular. The psalmist may be exhorting himself or another, but it seems likely that it is the former. In both, the psalmist refers to himself in the first couple of verses and then changes to second person singular. In both, he comforts with the promises of God. "Surely he will deliver you from the snare of the fowler, From the calamitous pestilence" (Ps. 91:3–13). "He will not permit your foot to be moved; He who keeps you will not slumber" (Ps. 121:3–8).

In Psalm 52, David speaks directly to one particular person, Doeg the Edomite, who, at the orders of King Saul, slaughtered the priests of Nob (1 Sam. 22:6–19). "Why do you boast in mischief, O mighty man? . . . God will likewise destroy you forever." He names Doeg in the heading but not in the body of the psalm and does not mention Doeg's specific crime. Therefore, the psalm is applicable in many other situations that God's people encounter even today. Psalm 55:12–13 is another example. David was probably thinking of Ahithophel (2 Sam. 15:31), but Judas did the same thing to our Lord, and many of us have also experienced betrayal by friends.

Psalm 128 is for heads of households: "Your wife will be like a fruitful vine inside your house, Your sons like olive plants around your table." Perhaps the same is true of Psalm 127:2: "It is vain for you to rise up early, To sit up late, To eat the bread of sorrows. Thus He will give to His beloved sleep."

The sons of Korah composed Psalm 45, "A Song of Loves" (cf. the heading) celebrating the wedding of the king and his queen. The meaning of the song shines fully only in light of Paul's exhortations to husbands and wives: "This is a great mystery, but I speak concerning Christ and the church" (Eph. 5:32). Hebrews 1 also interprets verses 6–7 as prophetic of the exaltation of Christ.

Psalms 58 and 82 warn wicked judges and rulers to judge righteously. Psalm 2:10–12 commands them to kiss the Son lest they perish from the way when His wrath is kindled. Psalm 4:2–5 addresses sons of men. The Hebrew has two phrases, which some translations confuse: "sons of man" and "sons of men." "Sons of man" refers to men in general, and "sons of men" refers to nobles. In Psalm 4, David is talking about nobles who abuse the wealth (or glory) that God has given them, and he says of himself that he has more gladness than when their grain and wine increased.

There are many psalms that address our fellow saints. In some we do it together: "Sing aloud to God our strength" (Ps. 81). In others we speak as individuals to the rest of God's people: "O magnify Yahweh with me" (Ps. 34:3).

These psalms are usually songs of exhortation, instruction, or encouragement. "Come, behold the works of Yahweh, What desolations He has appointed in the earth" (Ps. 46:8). "Walk around Zion" (Ps. 48:12). "Yahweh remembers us: He will bless" (Ps. 115:12). Psalm 37 is a long exhortation not to fret about the prosperity of the wicked. Psalm 78 begins with the exhortation, "Give ear, O my people," and warns them against unfaithfulness by reciting what happened to Ephraim who "turned back in the day of battle." Psalm 107 is a calling to men to praise the Lord for His goodness and concludes on a didactic note: "Who is wise and will observe these things? Even they will understand the lovingkindness of Yahweh." In Psalms 111, 112, and 113 we call others to praise. In Psalm 122 we urge them to pray for Jerusalem.

Enemies receive many words of warning and condemnation. "How long will you assail a man? You will be slain, all of you" (Ps. 62:3). "Depart from me, you evildoers" (Ps. 119:115; cf. Ps. 6:8; 139:19). "How can you say to my soul, 'Flee to your mountain like a bird?'" (Ps. 11:1).

What will be given to you?
And what will be added to you,
O treacherous tongue?
Sharpened arrows of a warrior
With coals of broom trees.

—Ps. 120:3–4

Psalms 47, 66:1–5, 96, 97, 98, 99, 100, and 117 call the nations to praise the Lord. They anticipate the addition of the Gentiles to the people of God after the ascension of Christ.

Psalm 49 urges all people—low and high, rich and poor—not to trust in riches and warns in the starkest language those who think their houses will last forever. Psalm 150 calls on all who have breath to praise the Lord.

Psalm 29 addresses the sons of the mighty. Many think these are angels, but even if they are not, other psalms do the same (cf. Ps. 103:20–22; 148:2).

The psalms sometimes personify inanimate creatures and speak to them. They can neither hear nor respond, but they do have their place and purpose in the kingdom of God. Psalm 24 commands the gates of Jerusalem to open before the victorious king. Psalm 114 asks the hills and mountains why they skipped like lambs before the Lord. It recalls Mount Sinai and Israel's sojourn in the wilderness. Psalm 148 summons all creatures—animate and inanimate, in heaven and on earth—to praise the Lord.

The audiences of the psalms cover the whole range of God's creatures, many different groups of people both righteous and wicked, and even angels. Sometimes God Himself speaks to them through us, as in Psalm 60:6–8:

God has spoken in his holiness:
"I will rejoice;
I will divide Shechem
And measure out the Valley of Succoth.
Gilead is Mine."

At other times we use our own words, or rather the words that God inspired His servants to write for us, as in Psalm 66:1: "Make a joyful shout to God, all the earth!"

The psalms are full of admonition, encouragement, exhortation, instruction, warning, threat, and promise for all God's creatures. In fact, almost any kind of speech belonging to plain words is also a subject in one or more psalms.

Conclusion

We often hear that worship is a dialogue between ourselves and God. It is also, at least in the singing of psalms, conversation we have among ourselves in God's presence. We find in the Book of Psalms an intricate web of speakers and audiences. God is the primary speaker and the primary audience. Paul even adds to the exhortation in Colossians 3: "singing with grace in your hearts to the Lord." But our brothers and sisters are secondary, and others outside the church come after them.

The people of God gather in the presence of God to worship. While they are there, God in Christ speaks to them, and they speak to Him. But while God listens, they also speak to themselves, to each other, and to the angels who are present. And sometimes they turn outward, as it were, and speak to the world around them.

This speaking is not a free-for-all. We stand in the presence of our King. Our first duty is silence so we may hear Him: "Yahweh is in His holy temple. Let all the earth be silent before Him" (Hab. 2:20). We must be swift to hear and slow to speak (James 1:19). When we do speak, it must be carefully, under the direction of the King, using words that are pleasing to Him for the purposes He ordained. The psalms ensure that we are singing nothing but what He has given us to say.

While we sing the psalms, we should be aware who we are talking to, why we are talking, and what we are saying. Do we speak to God? Fear Him. To ourselves? Be careful to hear. To fellow saints? Do it with love. To nations, enemies, or rulers? Let it be with boldness, for by the Word we bind kings with chains and nobles with fetters of iron (Ps. 149:8). To heaven, earth, and other creatures? The whole creation groans with us under the bondage of corruption and will participate in the glorious liberty of the sons of God (Rom. 8:19–22). By singing thus we glorify God our Savior and edify each other.

But others also speak to us even while we are speaking to them, so there must be care both to speak and to hear well. When singing the psalms, we do not sing alone but with a vast and varied host. Psalm 148 first calls on the heavenly host, angels, sun and moon, stars, heavens, and waters above the heavens to praise Him. Then it summons the great host of earthly creatures: sea creatures and depths, fire and hail, snow, clouds and wind, mountains and hills, trees and cedars, beasts and cattle, creeping things and birds, kings and all peoples, princes and all judges, young men and maidens, old men and children:

Let them praise the name of Yahweh,
For His name alone is exalted;
His glory is above the earth and heaven.

If we sing with all these, should we not—sometimes at the very least—sing the songs that God gave to both them and us and that they themselves have learned?

Appendix 2

SOME OTHER OBJECTIONS TO THE PSALMS

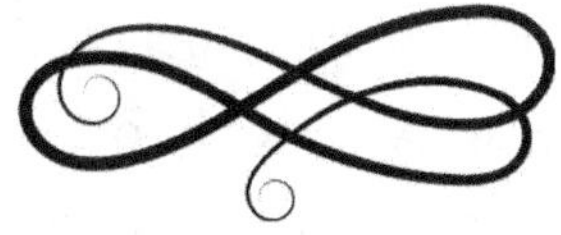

This book has addressed perhaps the most significant objection to using the psalms in public and private worship: that they do not talk enough about Christ. This appendix will look briefly at some other objections.

The first objection is that they are difficult to understand. Hymns, especially those from the nineteenth century onward, are almost always readily accessible to us. We can sing them with immediate understanding. The psalms are more difficult. They are sometimes obscure in their references to Old Testament history, ceremonies, and institutions. They do not express ideas in contemporary forms and words. The flow of thought is different. A perceived lack of connection between verses or paragraphs confuses. Other points could be made, but their difficulty to us of the twenty-first century is undeniable.

There is only one solution to this problem: to become better acquainted with them by making a deliberate choice to study them and use them despite their difficulties. That requires an effort that many may not be willing to make, but it will reap a rich reward in spiritual growth and maturity.

Second, the psalms are filled with imprecations and hatred for the enemies of God. That makes us uncomfortable at best. Some have called them sub-Christian, or even anti-Christian. Some who sing the psalms regularly avoid the use of such imprecatory psalms such as Psalms 109 and 137 and skip over imprecatory verses in other psalms.

I know this difficulty from personal experience. The problem is not with God's inspired Word but with us. Our discomfort with these psalms may be due to various reasons: (1) we are not enough advanced in sanctification; (2) our love for God and His church falls short of the standard set in Psalm 137; (3) we are not mature enough to understand how such psalms fit into the whole pattern of Christian living; or (4) we are too much influenced by a man-centered rather than a God-centered theology.

The psalms are very deeply rooted in antithetical thinking; that is, in the awareness of the great gulf between the world and the people of God. God Himself created it when He put enmity between the seed of the woman and the seed of the serpent (Gen. 3:15). Almost all the psalms contain an antithetical element. Psalm 1 is about the difference between the practice and destinies of the righteous and wicked. Psalm 2 is about the Lord's derision for those who try to cast off the yoke of His Anointed. Psalm 3 is about confidence in the Lord despite "ten thousands of people that have set themselves against me round about." We could go on almost indefinitely. The nations (or Gentiles) appear repeatedly in the psalms as our enemies against whom we pray. We must hasten to add, however, that we also call them to worship (Ps. 117) and expect the Lord to save them (Ps. 67).

This antithetical thinking should be part of the basic shape of our minds as long as we live in the world. It is not. We have become too worldly. We have forgotten the words of James 4:4: "You adulterers and adulteresses! Do you not know that the friendship of the world is enmity with God? Whoever therefore wants to be a friend of the world shows himself an enemy of God."

So we must learn again to think antithetically. Rising persecution will help. The world is displaying more openly its fundamental hatred of God and righteousness. This will force our attention to the hostility of our environment, and we will begin to look again to the Word of God, especially the Book of Psalms, to express our distresses and hopes to the God who hates all workers of iniquity (Ps. 5:5).

Third, in the psalms we sing about many things that we do not sing about in hymns or contemporary music. Nineteenth century hymns tend to focus on Christ my Savior and my personal experience of salvation (another reason we find them so readily accessible). Contemporary music is often about working up an emotional high. Both focus on positive things and positive feelings. The psalms also can be very personal. Psalm 23 is a wonderful example. They are also emotional, but the emotions are almost as frequently negative as they are positive—sorrow, anger, doubt, and fear appear along with confidence, joy, and hope. They include instruction, admonition, complaint, confessions of sin, and everything that belongs to our lives as Christians in a fallen world. Their language is sometimes homely rather than exalted; bottles and beds; noses, bellies, hairy scalps, legs, and fat hearts; worms, dogs, bulls with gaping mouths, and roaring lions; backbiting tongues and bribes; wickedness, sadness, death and sickness, and all kinds of things that are either unpleasant or too ordinary for the high art of praise. We must expand our understanding of what subjects are appropriate for song and get used to a certain earthiness that we do not usually find in manmade songs.

Another problem is that the psalms use very bold language. Why do You stand far off? How long will You forget me? Why do You sleep? Wake up! How long will You look on? Make haste! Bow down Your ear. You have struck my enemies on the jaw. He flew upon the wings of the wind. The Lord shall swallow them in His wrath. Judge me, O God. You have examined me and found nothing. His eyelids test the sons of men. Why do you fume with envy, you mountains of many peaks? Let the rivers clap their hands. We are more timid and less colorful in our songs and prayers. Some things seem irreverent, some impossible, and others preposterous. We need better comprehension and bolder faith.

Fourth, we think differently about music than the authors of the psalms and Christians in other ages. Referring to Ephesians 5:18–20 and Colossians 3:16, Calvin Stapert, professor of music emeritus at Calvin College, says:

> Clear as these passages are in declaring that Christian singing is a response to the Word of Christ and to being filled with the Spirit, it is hard to keep from turning the cause and effect around. Music, with its stimulating power, can too easily be seen as the cause and the "Spirit filling" as the effect.[6]

And again,

> Those misled by this kind of epiclesis think—or at least act as though—we convene ourselves [for worship] and then wait for God to show up because we have said the magic words or cranked up enough volume in our praise. They also inevitably blame the music when they feel worship to be joyless and spiritless. They see music as a stimulus to rather than a vehicle for the expression of joy, an enticement for the Spirit's presence rather than a grateful response for it, as though the Spirit were at the beck and call of our music.[7]

---

[6] Calvin R. Stapert, *A New Song for an Old World* (William B. Eerdmans Publishing Company, 2007), 20.

[7] Stabert, *A New Song for an Old World*, 202.

The psalms are clearly response rather than enticement. To the psalmists, their songs were offerings (the calves of their lips, Hos. 14:2, KJV) made to the God into whose presence they had come.

Enter His gates with thanksgiving,
His courts with praise.
Be thankful to Him. Bless His name.
For Yahweh is good;
To everlasting is His lovingkindness,
And to generation after generation His faithfulness.

These are difficulties, but they are not insurmountable. They require study, but study of the Word always reaps a rich harvest of blessing.

ACKNOWLEDGMENTS

Fervent thanks to my friends and brothers in Christ, Dr. David Sills, Rev. Sam Waltman, and Mr. David Sawyer for their gracious help in the editing of the manuscript. They made many contributions and gave much encouragement.

www.ingramcontent.com/pod-product-compliance
Lightning Source LLC
LaVergne TN
LVHW020637100826
845148LV00012B/2211

* 9 7 9 8 9 0 3 4 4 0 1 4 6 *